D1682702

9781557382801

1 · 9 · 9 · 2

STOCK · TRADER'S

ALMANAC

BY YALE HIRSCH

ANNIVERSARY

PRESIDENTIAL · ELECTION YEAR · EDITION

THE HIRSCH ORGANIZATION INC. • SIX DEER TRAIL • OLD TAPPAN NJ 07675

This Twenty-Fifth Edition is respectfully dedicated
to

Victor Sperandeo

His book "Methods of a Wall Street Master" proves that he is indeed
"the ultimate Wall Street pro." We have selected it as
the Best Investment Book for 1992.

The Stock Trader's Almanac is an organizer. It puts investing on a business
basis **by making things easier**.

1. It is a monthly reminder and refresher course.

2. It updates investment knowledge; informs you of new techniques and tools.

3. It alerts you to seasonal opportunities and dangers.

4. It provides an historical viewpoint by providing pertinent statistics on past market behavior.

5. It supplies every form needed for portfolio-planning, record-keeping and tax preparation.

For several years prior to the publication of our first **Stock Trader's Almanac**, we collected items from financial columns, books and articles that pointed to seasonal tendencies in the stock market. It occurred to us that these intriguing phenomena should be thoroughly researched and arranged in calendar order. So we did it! We also examined various investment, record-keeping forms and found some hadn't been updated for 20-30 years. Others were so cumbersome they were beyond anyone's patience. So we designed new and more practical forms.

We are constantly searching for new insights and nuances about the stock market and welcome any suggestions from our readers.

Have a healthy and prosperous 1992!

This symbol signifies THIRD FRIDAY OF THE MONTH on calendar pages and tells you to be alert to extraordinary volatility due to expiration of index future contracts. Triple-witching days appear during March, June, September and December.

INTRODUCTION
TO THE
TWENTY-FIFTH EDITION

It is with a great feeling of celebration that I introduce the Twenty-Fifth annual edition of **The Stock Trader's Almanac**. I am pleased and proud to have brought significant and useful information to investors over the years. This edition, as well as those that follow, continues in that tradition.

J.P. Morgan's classic retort when questioned about the future course of the stock market was, ''Stocks will fluctuate.'' This remark is often quoted with a wink-of-the-eye implication that the only prediction one can truly make about the market is that it will go up, down, or sideways. Many investors wholeheartedly believe that no one ever really knows which way the market will go. Nothing could be further from the truth—as Almanac readers well know.

During the past twenty-five years I have made many exceptionally accurate forecasts in the **Stock Trader's Almanac**. These forecasts were based on thousands of hours of research into recurring patterns. I learned that while stocks do indeed fluctuate, they do so in well-defined, often predictable patterns which recur too frequently to be the result of chance or coincidence.

The Almanac is a practical working tool. Its wealth of information is organized on a calendar basis. It alerts you to those little-known market patterns and tendencies on which shrewd professionals maximize profit potential. You will be able to forecast market trends with accuracy and confidence when you use the Almanac to help you understand:

1. How our quadrennial presidential elections unequivocally affect the economy and the stock market—just as the moon affects the tides.

2. That there is significant market bias at certain times of the day, week, month and year.

3. How the passage of the Twentieth Amendment to the Constitution fathered the January Barometer which has a super record for predicting the course of the stock market each year.

4. Just how important it is to be a contrarian.

Many investors have made fortunes following the political cycle. You can be certain that money managers who control hundreds of millions of dollars are also political cycle watchers. Sharp people are not likely to ignore a pattern that has been working like a charm for decades.

Even if you are an investor who pays scant attention to cycles, indicators and patterns, your investment survival could hinge on your interpretation of one of the recurring patterns found within these pages. One of the most intriguing and important patterns is the symbiotic relationship between Washington and Wall Street. Aside from the potential profitability in seasonal patterns, there's the pure joy of seeing the market very often do just what you expected.

To be short the market throughout all of 1992 would be a poor strategy. Incumbent presidents have tried to hold onto the White House sixteen times in this century and the market rose in thirteen election years. There were only three declining years: during World War 1 in 1916, during World War 2 in 1940 (both incumbents won re-election anyway), and during the worldwide depression in 1932 (Hoover lost).

3

THE 1992 STOCK TRADER'S ALMANAC

CONTENTS

DIRECTORY OF SEASONAL TRADING PATTERNS

STRATEGY, PLANNING & RECORD SECTION

1992 STRATEGY CALENDAR
(Option expiration dates encircled)

	MONDAY	TUESDAY	WEDNESDAY	THURSDAY	FRIDAY	SAT	SUN
JANUARY	30	31	1 JANUARY New Year's Day	2	3	4	5
	6	7	8	9	10	11	12
	13	14	15	16	(17)	18	19
	20 Martin Luther King Day	21	22	23	24	25	26
	27	28	29	30	31	1 FEBRUARY	2
FEBRUARY	3	4	5	6	7	8	9
	10	11	12 Lincoln's Birthday	13	14	15	16
	17 President's Day	18	19	20	(21)	22	23
	24	25	26	27	28	29	1 MARCH
MARCH	2	3	4 Ash Wednesday	5	6	7	8
	9	10	11	12	13	14	15
	16	17 St. Patrick's Day	18	19	(20)	21	22
	23	24	25	26	27	28	29
APRIL	30	31	1 APRIL	2	3	4	5
	6	7	8	9	10	11	12
	13	14	15	(16)	17 Good Friday	18 Passover	19 Easter
	20	21	22	23	24	25	26
	27	28	29	30	1 MAY	2	3
MAY	4	5	6	7	8	9	10 Mother's Day
	11	12	13	14	(15)	16	17
	18	19	20	21	22	23	24
	25 Memorial Day	26	27	28	29	30	31
JUNE	1 JUNE	2	3	4	5	6	7
	8	9	10	11	12	13	14
	15	16	17	18	(19)	20	21 Father's Day
	22	23	24	25	26	27	28

1992 STRATEGY CALENDAR
(Option expiration dates encircled)

MONDAY	TUESDAY	WEDNESDAY	THURSDAY	FRIDAY	SAT	SUN	
29	30	1 JULY	2	3	4 Independence Day	5	JULY
6	7	8	9	10	11	12	
13	14	15	16	(17)	18	19	
20	21	22	23	24	25	26	
27	28	29	30	31	1 AUGUST	2	
3	4	5	6	7	8	9	AUGUST
10	11	12	13	14	15	16	
17	18	19	20	(21)	22	23	
24	25	26	27	28	29	30	
31	1 SEPTEMBER	2	3	4	5	6	SEPTEMBER
7 Labor Day	8	9	10	11	12	13	
14	15	16	17	(18)	19	20	
21	22	23	24	25	26	27	
28 Rosh Hashana	29	30	1 OCTOBER	2	3	4	OCTOBER
5	6	7 Yom Kippur	8	9	10	11	
12 Columbus Day	13	14	15	(16)	17	18	
19	20	21	22	23	24	25	
26	27	28	29	30	31	1 NOVEMBER	
2	3 Election Day	4	5	6	7	8	NOVEMBER
9	10	11 Veteran's Day	12	13	14	15	
16	17	18	19	(20)	21	22	
23	24	25	26 Thanksgiving	27	28	29	
30	1 DECEMBER	2	3	4	5	6	DECEMBER
7	8	9	10	11	12	13	
14	15	16	17	(18)	19	20 Hanukkah	
21	22	23	24	25 Christmas	26	27	
28	29	30	31				

20th Amendment made "Lame Ducks" disappear
Now, "As January goes, so goes the year"

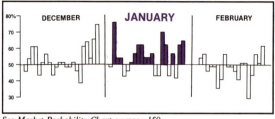

JANUARY ALMANAC

JANUARY							FEBRUARY						
S	M	T	W	T	F	S	S	M	T	W	T	F	S
				1	2	3							1
4	5	6	7	8	9	10	2	3	4	5	6	7	8
11	12	13	14	15	16	17	9	10	11	12	13	14	15
18	19	20	21	22	23	24	16	17	18	19	20	21	22
25	26	27	28	29	30	31	23	24	25	26	27	28	29

See Market Probability Chart on page 159.

☐ As January goes, so goes the year (pgs. 10-22) ☐ Greatest concentration of turndowns since 1949 occurred in month's first six trading days ☐ Worst five Dow losers tend to outperform best five in last-through-the-first weeks of year ☐ January Barometer outperforms all other monthly barometers in predicting the next 11 months ☐ Most volatile month, highest average point change ☐ Low-priced stocks beat quality in early weeks of year ☐ Only one strong January in last five second-term re-election victories.

JANUARY DAILY POINT CHANGES DOW JONES INDUSTRIALS

Previous Month Close	1982	1983	1984	1985	1986	1987	1988	1989	1990	1991
	875.00	1046.54	1258.64	1211.57	1546.67	1895.95	1938.83	2168.57	2753.20	2633.66
1	H	H	H	H	H	H	H	H	H	H
2	—	—	—	—12.70	— 8.94	—31.36	—	—	56.95	—23.02
3	—	—19.50	— 5.90	— 9.05	11.47	—	—	—23.93	— 0.42	—37.13
4	7.52	19.04	16.31	— 4.86	— 1.61	—	76.42	33.04	— 13.65	— 7.42
5	—17.22	— 1.19	13.19	—	—	44.01	16.25	12.86	— 22.83	—
6	— 4.28	26.03	4.40	—	—	3.51	6.30	3.75	—	—
7	0.76	5.15	—	5.63	18.12	19.12	14.09	—	—	—43.32
8	4.75	—	—	1.11	—39.10	8.30	—140.58	—	21.12	—13.36
9	—	—	— 0.42	11.04	— 8.38	3.66	—	5.17	— 28.37	—39.11
10	—	16.28	— 7.74	20.76	— 4.70	—	—	— 6.25	— 15.36	28.46
11	—16.07	— 8.56	— 1.16	— 5.41	—	—	33.82	13.22	10.03	2.73
12	— 2.76	— 0.18	1.99	—	—	3.51	— 16.58	15.89	— 71.46	—
13	— 8.75	— 9.66	— 9.21	—	7.00	3.52	— 3.82	3.75	—	—
14	3.33	6.90	—	16.45	— 1.49	22.07	— 8.62	—	—	—17.58
15	5.32	—	—	— 3.75	8.25	35.72	39.96	—	— 19.84	6.68
16	—	—	2.51	— 0.11	14.34	5.90	—	— 1.43	23.25	18.32
17	—	3.96	3.87	— 1.99	— 4.93	—	—	—10.00	— 33.49	114.60
18	7.52	— 5.16	— 2.09	— 1.33	—	—	7.79	24.11	7.25	23.27
19	— 7.71	—11.59	— 3.35	—	—	25.87	— 27.52	0.36	11.52	—
20	— 1.52	2.76	— 6.91	—	— 7.57	1.97	57.20	— 3.75	—	—
21	2.38	—17.84	—	34.01	—14.68	—10.40	0.17	—	—	—17.57
22	— 3.24	—	—	— 1.87	—12.16	51.60	24.20	—	— 77.45	—25.99
23	—	—	—14.66	15.23	8.95	—44.15	—	—16.97	14.87	15.84
24	—	—22.81	— 1.57	— 4.30	18.69	—	—	38.04	— 10.82	24.01
25	— 2.28	11.86	—10.99	5.63	—	—	42.94	9.45	— 43.46	16.34
26	— 1.24	— 4.04	— 2.20	—	—	5.76	25.86	25.18	— 1.81	—
27	1.15	25.66	0.31	—	7.68	43.17	— 9.45	31.79	—	—
28	21.59	1.10	—	1.77	18.81	12.94	18.90	—	—	— 4.95
29	6.85	—	—	14.79	2.52	— 3.38	28.18	—	— 5.85	8.16
30	—	—	— 8.48	— 4.74	— 6.76	— 1.97	—	1.25	— 10.14	50.50
31	—	10.95	— 0.94	— 1.11	18.81	—	—	18.21	47.30	23.27
Close	871.10	1075.70	1220.58	1286.77	1570.99	2158.04	1958.22	2342.32	2590.54	2736.39
Change	— 3.90	29.16	—38.06	75.20	24.32	262.09	19.39	173.75	—162.66	102.73

DEC/JANUARY

MONDAY
30

Get inside information from the president
and you will probably lose half your
money. If you get it from the chairman
of the board, you will lose all
of your money.
— Jim Rogers

TUESDAY
31

Coles House

Computer Setup & Proof of Payroll ~ 8hrs

Capitalism without bankruptcy is like
Christianity without hell.
— Frank Borman,
CEO, Eastern Airlines, April 1986

New Year's Day
(Market Closed)

WEDNESDAY
1

Management is always going to be biased,
either they're too close to the company
to see what's really going on, or
they're not totally upfront.
— Morton Davis
Chairman, D.H. Blair

THURSDAY
2

CHADWICK FUNERAL HOME

4TH PAYROLL TAXES &

COMPUTER SETUP

Billed
Payroll taxes

4 1/2 hrs

I'm always turned off by an overly
optimistic letter from the president in the
annual report. If his letter is mildly
pessimistic to me that's a good sign.
— Philip Carret

FRIDAY
3

When I talk to a company that tells me the
last analyst showed up three years ago, I
can hardly contain my enthusiasm.
— Peter Lynch

SATURDAY
4

ARDMORE BEVERAGE
PAYROLL

SUNDAY
5

THE INCREDIBLE JANUARY BAROMETER
ONLY THREE MAJOR ERRORS IN 41 YEARS

Nothing beats the January Barometer. Since 1950, no other indicator has predicted the annual course of the market with such accuracy. Based on whether Standard & Poor's composite index is up or down in January, most years have in essence followed suit—36 out of 41 times—for an 87% batting average. However, there were **no errors in odd years** when new congresses convened.

January performance chronologically and by rank is shown below. Except for 1987, note how the top 23 Januarys had gains of 1% and launched the best market years. January 1986 was affected by program trading. Twenty Januarys were losers or had minuscule gains. All bear markets were preceded or accompanied by inferior Januarys. Only one good year followed a January loss. 1966, 1968 and 1982 were significant errors—Vietnam affected the first two.

AS JANUARY GOES, SO GOES THE YEAR

Market Performance in January					January Performance by Rank		
Year	Previous Year's Close	January Close	January Change	Rank	Year	January Change	Year's Change
1950	16.76*	17.05*	1.7%	1.	1987	13.2%	2.0%
1951	20.41	21.66	6.1	2.	1975	12.3	31.5
1952	23.77	24.14	1.6	3.	1976	11.8	19.1
1953	26.57	26.38	−0.7	4.	1967	7.8	20.1
1954	24.81	26.08	5.1	5.	1985	7.4	26.3
1955	35.98	36.63	1.8	6.	1989	7.1	27.3
1956	45.48	43.82	−3.6	7.	1961	6.3	23.1
1957	46.67	44.72	−4.2	8.	1951	6.1	16.5
1958	39.99	41.70	4.3	9.	1980	5.8	25.8
1959	55.21	55.42	0.4	10.	1954	5.1	45.0
1960	59.89	55.61	−7.1	11.	1963	4.9	18.9
1961	58.11	61.78	6.3	12.	1958	4.3	38.1
1962	71.55	68.84	−3.8	13.	1991	4.2	??
1963	63.10	66.20	4.9	14.	1971	4.0	10.8
1964	75.02	77.04	2.7	15.	1979	4.0	12.3
1965	84.75	87.56	3.3	16.	1988	4.0	12.4
1966	92.43	92.88	0.5	17.	1983	3.3	17.3
1967	80.33	86.61	7.8	18.	1965	3.3	9.1
1968	96.47	92.24	−4.4	19.	1964	2.7	13.0
1969	103.86	103.01	−0.8	20.	1955	1.8	26.4
1970	92.06	85.02	−7.6	21.	1972	1.8	15.6
1971	92.15	95.88	4.0	22.	1950	1.7	21.8
1972	102.09	103.94	1.8	23.	1952	1.6	11.8
1973	118.05	116.03	−1.7	24.	1966	0.5	−13.1
1974	97.55	96.57	−1.0	25.	1959	0.4	8.5
1975	68.56	76.98	12.3	26.	1986	0.2	14.6
1976	90.19	100.86	11.8	27.	1953	−0.7	− 6.6
1977	107.46	102.03	−5.1	28.	1969	−0.8	−11.4
1978	95.10	89.25	−6.2	29.	1984	−0.9	1.4
1979	96.11	99.93	4.0	30.	1974	−1.0	−29.7
1980	107.94	114.16	5.8	31.	1973	−1.7	−17.4
1981	135.76	129.55	−4.6	32.	1982	−1.8	14.8
1982	122.55	120.40	−1.8	33.	1956	−3.6	2.6
1983	140.64	145.30	3.3	34.	1962	−3.8	−11.8
1984	164.93	163.41	−0.9	35.	1957	−4.2	−14.3
1985	167.24	179.63	7.4	36.	1968	−4.4	7.7
1986	211.28	211.78	0.2	37.	1981	−4.6	− 9.7
1987	242.17	274.08	13.2	38.	1977	−5.1	−11.5
1988	247.08	257.07	4.0	39.	1978	−6.2	1.1
1989	277.72	297.47	7.1	40.	1990	−6.9	− 6.6
1990	353.40	329.08	−6.9	41.	1960	−7.1	− 3.0
1991	330.22	343.93	4.2	42.	1970	−7.6	0.1

*S & P Composite Index

JANUARY

MONDAY 6 ✓

Chadwick Funeral Home
Payroll Tax Forms - 4th Qtr & Annual - 2HRS
Receivables & Auto Comp. - 2 HRS

Ardmore Beverage - W-2 & Assembly
1½ HRS

TUESDAY 7

YWBHA - Coles House

Kathleen - 8 HRS - Audit
MIS - 8 HRS = Payroll Taxes - Etc

WEDNESDAY 8

OTXMS 395   8 (2.8⁰)
(8)   = 395
              5 3/4

THURSDAY 9

1½·8⁰)

YWBHA - Coles House

Kathleen - 8 HRS - Audit
MIS - 8 HRS - Audit

FRIDAY 10

Chadwick

SATURDAY 11

J. Carver 11:00 AM

SUNDAY 12

JANUARY BAROMETER IN GRAPHIC FORM

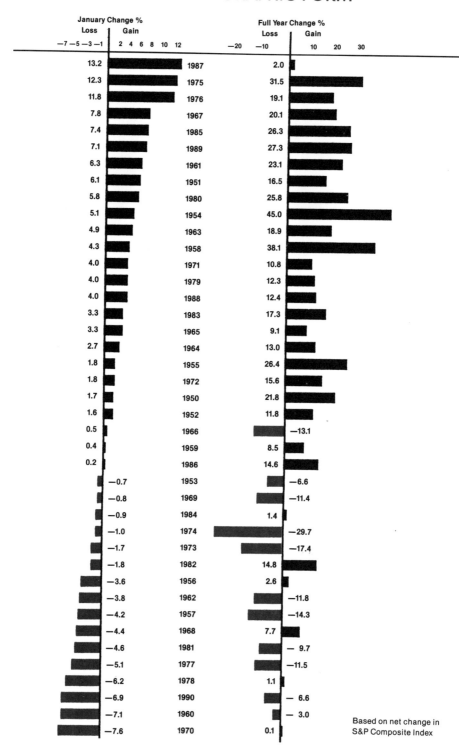

| January Change % | | | Full Year Change % | |
| Loss | Gain | | Loss | Gain |

Based on net change in
S&P Composite Index

JANUARY

MONDAY
13

The test of success is not what you do
when you are on top. Success is how high
you bounce when you hit bottom.
— General George S. Patton

TUESDAY
14

"When an old man dies,
a library burns down."
— an African motto

WEDNESDAY
15

YWBHA — 10.00 AM

Computer — Adjustment — 3 Hrs
& Report Review

Audit — Investment   4 Hrs

Do your work with your whole heart and
you will succeed — there is so
little competition.
— Elbert Hubbard

THURSDAY
16

The usual bull market successfully
weathers a number of tests until it is
considered invulnerable, whereupon
it is ripe for a bust.
— George Soros

FRIDAY
17

Jones Termite & Pest Control In.

Automobile — Fringe Benefits Calculation   1 Hr.

The people who sustain the worst losses
are usually those who overreach. And it's
not necessary: Steady, moderate gains
will get you where you want to go.
— John Train

SATURDAY
18

SUNDAY
19

JANUARY'S FIRST FIVE DAYS:
AN "EARLY WARNING" SYSTEM

January followers can often get a glimpse of what lies ahead by watching the market's action during the first five trading days of the month. These five days serve as an excellent "early warning" system with a batting average almost equal to the January Barometer's 87%.

Early January gains since 1950 were matched by whole-year gains with just two exceptions, both Vietnam related: The start of the war triggered big military spending which delayed the start of the 1966 bear market; and the imminence of a final ceasefire raised stock prices temporarily in early January 1973. Fifteen Januarys got off to a bad start and eight of those years ended on the downside. The seven that didn't follow suit were 1955, 1956, 1978, 1982, 1985, 1986, 1988 and both 1956 and 1978 were only up a smidgen.

Despite a good record, remember that five days is a brief span and some extraordinary event could sidetrack this indicator which the infamous program traders did on 1986's fifth day and again on 1990's fifth day.

THE FIRST-FIVE-DAYS-IN-JANUARY INDICATOR

| | Chronologic Data | | | | | Ranked By Performance | |
| | Previous Year's | 5th Day in | Change 1st 5 | | | | Change 1st 5 | Change For |
Year	Close	January	Days		Rank	Year	Days	Year
1950	16.76*	17.09*	2.0%		1.	1987	6.2%	2.0%
1951	20.41	20.88	2.3		2.	1976	4.9	19.1
1952	23.77	23.91	0.6		3.	1983	3.1	17.3
1953	26.57	26.33	−0.9		4.	1967	3.1	20.1
1954	24.81	24.93	0.5		5.	1979	2.8	12.3
1955	35.98	35.33	−1.8		6.	1963	2.6	18.9
1956	45.48	44.51	−2.1		7.	1958	2.5	38.1
1957	46.67	46.25	−0.9		8.	1984	2.4	1.4
1958	39.99	40.99	2.5		9.	1951	2.3	16.5
1959	55.21	55.40	0.3		10.	1975	2.2	31.5
1960	59.89	59.50	−0.7		11.	1950	2.0	21.8
1961	58.11	58.81	1.2		12.	1973	1.5	−17.4
1962	71.55	69.12	−3.4		13.	1972	1.4	15.6
1963	63.10	64.74	2.6		14.	1964	1.3	13.0
1964	75.02	76.00	1.3		15.	1961	1.2	23.1
1965	84.75	85.37	0.7		16.	1989	1.2	27.3
1966	92.43	93.14	0.8		17.	1980	0.9	25.8
1967	80.33	82.81	3.1		18.	1966	0.8	−13.1
1968	96.47	96.62	0.2		19.	1965	0.7	9.1
1969	103.86	100.80	−2.9		20.	1970	0.7	0.1
1970	92.06	92.68	0.7		21.	1952	0.6	11.8
1971	92.15	92.19	0.0		22.	1954	0.5	45.0
1972	102.09	103.47	1.4		23.	1959	0.3	8.5
1973	118.05	119.85	1.5		24.	1968	0.2	7.7
1974	97.55	96.12	−1.5		25.	1990	0.1	− 6.6
1975	68.56	70.04	2.2		26.	1971	0.0	10.8
1976	90.19	94.58	4.9		27.	1960	−0.7	− 3.0
1977	107.46	105.01	−2.3		28.	1953	−0.9	− 6.6
1978	95.10	90.69	−4.6		29.	1957	−0.9	−14.3
1979	96.11	98.80	2.8		30.	1974	−1.5	−29.7
1980	107.94	108.95	0.9		31.	1988	−1.5	12.4
1981	135.76	133.06	−2.0		32.	1986	−1.6	14.6
1982	122.55	119.55	−2.4		33.	1955	−1.8	26.4
1983	140.64	145.18	3.2		34.	1985	−1.9	26.3
1984	164.93	168.90	2.4		35.	1981	−2.0	− 9.7
1985	167.24	163.99	−1.9		36.	1956	−2.1	2.6
1986	211.28	207.97	−1.6		37.	1977	−2.3	−11.5
1987	242.17	257.28	6.2		38.	1982	−2.4	14.8
1988	247.08	243.40	−1.5		39.	1969	−2.9	−11.4
1989	277.72	280.98	1.2		40.	1962	−3.4	−11.8
1990	353.40	353.79	0.1		41.	1978	−4.6	1.1
1991	330.22	314.88	−4.6		42.	1991	−4.6	??

1992 417.09

416 50

*S & P Composite Index

JANUARY

MONDAY 20

Jones Termite 10:00 AM

(B) (P)

8r 22387 -7502
Jr. 12127 -10116 -2111

Payroll Tax Set & Forms 4 Hrs
Proof of Cash/General Ledger 4 Hrs
Analysis of Accounts 2 Hrs

The best time to buy long-term bonds is
when short-term rates are higher than
long-term rates.
— George Soros

TUESDAY 21

Most periodicals and trade journals are
deadly dull, and indeed full of fluff
provided by public relations agents.
— Jim Rogers

WEDNESDAY 22

Tax Forms Symposium -

A poor stock market will discourage both
consumer and business outlays. Also a
decline in the value of stocks reduces their
value as collateral, a further depressant.
— George Soros

THURSDAY 23

Tax Forms Symposium

I imagine one of the reasons people cling
to their hates so stubbornly is because they
sense, once hate is gone, they will be
forced to deal with pain.
— James Baldwin,
1955, *Notes of a Native Son*

FRIDAY 24

Jones Termite & Pest Control

Depreciation, 8 Hrs
Amortization
Journal Entries,
Telephone, etc.

21624500

I never hired anybody who wasn't smarter
than me.
— Don Hewett, Producer, *60 Minutes*

SATURDAY 25

Jones Termite

Worksheet 2 Hr

SUNDAY 26

BEAT THE DOW WITH ONE ARM TIED BEHIND YOUR BACK

A single observation by Michael O'Higgins has resulted in, "Beating the Dow," published in 1991 by HarperCollins $19.95. The book presents a very simple system any investor can use to outperform the stock market.

TEN HIGHEST YIELDERS

Investing in the ten highest-yielding Dow Jones industrial stocks at the start of each year between 1973 and 1989 produced a cumulative total gain of 1553%, a 17.9% annual compounded return. The Dow average of 30 industrials during this 17-year period gained 499%, or 11.1% annually.

FIVE LOWEST-PRICED

Choosing just the five lowest-priced issues among the ten highest yielders each year resulted in a 2401% total return, equal to 20.9% per year.

SECOND LOWEST-PRICED

Remarkably, picking one Dow stock each year, the second lowest-priced stock of the ten highest yielders, did best of all, a 4210% return, or 24.8% a year.

Isn't it amazing, that you can beat the Dow from within, using a few of its own components? O'Higgins has tried a number of variations, lowest P/E ratios, worst performers, lowest price/sales ratios, etc.

STRONGEST PERFORMERS

The best strategy used the five lowest-priced stocks from the ten highest-yielding Dow stocks that had outperformed the Dow average in the preceding year. An investment in these, a maximum of three stocks a year gained 3529% for the 17-year period, or a compounded annual return of 23.5%. Not bad! Name one mutual fund that has done this well!

A SIMPLE BEATING-THE-DOW SYSTEM (1973-1989)

	Total Return	Annual Return
30 Dow Jones industrials	499%	11.1%
10 highest-yielding Dow stocks	1553%	17.9%
5 lowest-priced of 10 high yielders	2401%	20.9%
Strongest performers of 5 low-priced	3529%	23.5%
2nd lowest-priced of 10 high yielders	4210%	24.8%

TWO WEEKS EACH YEAR AVERAGE 5.3%

Want an interesting way to average 5.3% for a particular two-week period every year? O'Higgins shows that investing in the five worst Dow losers prior to the fifth from the last trading day in December and getting out on the fourth trading day in January has produced this 5.3% return for the past 15 years.

Murphy Slate Mileage   # 22040391

MONDAY
27

*Law of destiny: Glory may be fleeting
but obscurity is forever.
— From A Traders Astrological Almanac*

Ywett A - THRS { 3 HRS } PAYROLL + W-2 ETC
{ 4 HRS - AUDIT

TUESDAY
28

22898705

*Let him that would move the world, first
move himself.
— Socrates*

Jones Termite & Pest Control
Tax Return Assembly   2 Hrs

WEDNESDAY
29

*When love and skill work together, expect
a masterpiece.
— John Ruskin*

Jones Termite + Pest Control
Post Journal Entries   3 1/2 Hrs
Close G/L
Set up new year
Misc. Review. etc

THURSDAY
30

*There is nothing good or bad, only
thinking makes it so.
— William Shakespeare*

FRIDAY
31

*You can't turn back the clock, but you can
wind it up again.
— Bonnie Pruden*

Jones Termite - Worksheet & Form 1120S - X Hrs

SATURDAY
1

SUNDAY
2

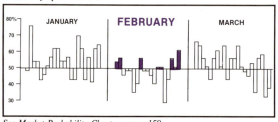

Big January moves ebb when they spill into Feb

See Market Probability Chart on page 159.

FEBRUARY ALMANAC

FEBRUARY						
S	M	T	W	T	F	S
						1
2	3	4	5	6	7	8
9	10	11	12	13	14	15
16	17	18	19	20	21	22
23	24	25	26	27	28	29

MARCH						
S	M	T	W	T	F	S
1	2	3	4	5	6	7
8	9	10	11	12	13	14
15	16	17	18	19	20	21
22	23	24	25	26	27	28
29	30	31				

□ Sharp January moves tend to consolidate in February □ If January is up, stay in; if down, move to sidelines □ RECORD: S&P 22 up, 20 down □ Best gains in 1970 (5.3%), 1975 (6.0%) and 1986 (7.1%) □ February's average change is −0.1%, third worst month since 1950 (pg. 38) □ Many analysts may revise annual forecasts at the beginning of February, as the rest of the year tends to follow the lead of January's performance, especially in odd years □ Worst election-year month, down four times out of last six.

FEBRUARY DAILY POINT CHANGES DOW JONES INDUSTRIALS

Previous Month	1982	1983	1984	1985	1986	1987	1988	1989	1990	1991
Close	871.10	1075.70	1220.58	1286.77	1570.99	2158.04	1958.22	2342.32	2590.54	2736.39
1	−19.41	−15.91	− 8.27	− 9.05	—		−13.59	− 4.11	− 4.28	− 5.70
2	0.86	2.85	1.57	—	—	21.38	8.29	− 4.46	16.44	—
3	− 7.52	2.02	−16.85	—	23.28	−10.97	−28.35	− 2.50	—	—
4	2.00	13.25	—	12.36	− 1.04	22.78	− 1.00	—	—	41.59
5	4.00	—	—	− 4.85	− 0.11	10.26	−13.09	—	19.82	16.09
6	—	—	−22.72	− 4.64	7.57	−14.62	—	−10.18	−16.21	42.57
7	—	9.19	6.18	9.49	12.73	—	—	26.07	33.78	−20.30
8	−17.60	−11.77	−24.19	0.11	—	—	−14.76	− 3.93	4.28	20.05
9	− 2.86	− 7.91	− 3.56	—	—	−10.13	18.74	−20.17	3.83	—
10	6.09	20.33	7.96	—	12.96	−18.70	47.58	−36.97	—	—
11	− 1.99	1.25	—	−13.91	− 3.56	13.92	− 0.50	—	—	71.54
12	0.86	—	—	0.55	7.11	6.18	21.72	—	−29.06	−27.48
13	—	—	−10.57	21.31	15.14	17.57	—	− 3.57	4.96	34.41
14	—	10.60	13.71	−10.04	19.38	—	—	− 1.25	0.22	−31.93
15	H	− 4.00	− 5.13	− 5.86	—	—	H	22.68	25.23	57.42
16	− 2.47	− 5.67	− 3.77	—	—	H	22.71	7.50	−13.96	—
17	− 3.71	1.48	− 6.07	—	H	54.14	0.14	13.39	—	—
18	1.33	3.91	—	H	14.33	—	−14.58	—	—	H
19	4.66	—	—	− 1.43	−20.52	6.46	28.18	—	H	− 2.47
20	—	—	H	2.54	14.56	8.85	—	H	−38.74	−33.17
21	—	H	− 9.53	− 4.09	24.89	—	—	1.61	−13.29	− 7.18
22	−13.04	−12.42	− 5.13	− 3.20	—	—	25.70	−42.50	− 8.79	− 2.47
23	1.72	16.54	0.42	—	—	−18.70	− 1.17	5.53	−10.58	—
24	13.79	24.87	30.47	—	0.57	6.74	0.83	−43.92	—	—
25	− 0.95	− 0.87	—	1.66	− 5.62	2.96	−22.38	—	—	− 1.49
26	− 1.43	—	—	8.61	4.24	− 9.56	5.64	—	38.29	−23.27
27	—	—	14.86	− 5.08	17.09	7.31	—	4.82	14.64	24.51
28	—	− 8.32	−22.82	2.98	− 4.93	—	—	8.03	10.13	− 6.93
29			− 2.51				48.41			
Close	824.39	1112.62	1154.63	1284.01	1709.06	2223.99	2071.62	2258.39	2627.25	2882.18
Change	−46.71	36.92	−65.95	−2.76	138.07	65.95	113.40	−83.93	36.71	145.79

MONDAY

3

Jones Termite & Pest Control

4 Hours - Filled Pa. Return

The man who masters himself,
masters the universe.
— Robert Krausz

TUESDAY

4

Young Women's Boarding Home Assn.

Audit   8 Hrs

The measure of success is not whether
you have a tough problem to deal with,
but whether its the same problem
you had last year.
— John Foster Dulles

WEDNESDAY

5

34.96   31.25
31.34

26898013

Don't be scared to take big steps — you
can't cross a chasm in two small jumps.
— David Lloyd George

THURSDAY

6

2537983 7

Choose a job you love, and you will never
have to work a day in your life.
— Confucius

FRIDAY

7

Short End.

Gathered

25847482

I cannot give you a formula for success
but I can give you a formula for failure.
Try to please everybody.
— Herbert Swope

SATURDAY

8

F Shea - 11:00 AM

SUNDAY

9

1933 "LAME DUCK" AMENDMENT REASON JANUARY BAROMETER WORKS

Between 1901 and 1933 the market's direction in January was similar to that of the whole year 19 times and different 14 times. Comparing January to the 11 subsequent months, 16 were similar and 17 dissimilar.

A dramatic change occurred in 1934—the Twentieth Amendment to the Constitution! Since then it has essentially been "As January goes, so goes the year." January's direction has been correct 46 of the 57 years—or 80% of the time.

January Barometer (Odd Years)
LAME DUCK AMMENDMENT RATIFIED 1933
JANUARY BAROMETER IS BORN

January %Change	12 Month's %Change	Same	Opposite
– 4.2	41.2		1935
3.8	– 38.6		1937
– 6.9	– 5.4	1939	
– 4.8	– 17.9	1941	
7.2	19.4	1943	
1.4	30.7	1945	
2.4	0.0	1947	
0.1	10.3	1949	
6.1	16.5	1951	
– 0.7	– 6.9	1953	
1.8	26.4	1955	
– 4.2	– 14.3	1957	
0.4	8.5	1959	
6.3	23.1	1961	
4.9	18.9	1963	
3.3	9.1	1965	
7.8	20.1	1967	
– 0.8	– 11.4	1969	
4.0	10.8	1971	
– 1.7	– 17.4	1973	
12.3	31.5	1975	
– 5.1	– 11.5	1977	
4.0	12.3	1979	
– 4.6	– 9.7	1981	
3.3	17.3	1983	
7.4	26.3	1985	
13.2	2.0	1987	
7.1	27.3	1989	
4.2	??	1991	

12 month's % change includes January's % change after 1933, and applicable month's % change in prior years. Based on S&P 500

Prior to 1934, new Congresses generally convened the first Monday in December (except when new Presidents were inaugurated). Newly elected Senators and Representatives, did not take office until December of the following year, **13 months later**. Defeated Congressmen stayed in Congress for all of the following session. They were known as "lame ducks."

Since the Twentieth (Lame Duck) Amendment was ratified in 1933, Congress convenes January 3 and includes those members newly elected the previous November. Inauguration Day was also moved up from March 4 to January 20. As a result several events have been squeezed into January which affect our economy and our stock market and quite possibly those of many nations of the world. During January, Congress convenes, the President gives the State of the Union message, presents the annual budget and sets national goals and priorities. Switch these events to any other month and chances are the January Barometer would become a memory.

The table shows the January Barometer and its predecessors in odd years. In 1935 and 1937 the Democrats already had the most lopsided congressional margins in history, so when these two Congresses convened it was anticlimactic. The January Barometer in all subsequent odd years compiled a **perfect record**.

(continued on page 22)

FEBRUARY

MONDAY 10

26 230 8 53 *380 718*

call Tom

or Co 189

Under capitalism, the seller chases after the buyer, and that makes both of them work better; under socialism, the buyer chases the seller, and neither has time to work.
— Andrei Sakharov's Uncle Ivan

TUESDAY 11

Chadwick Funeral Home *6.0 ✓*

Journal Entries
Depreciation Schedule
Review differences

"Listen to the song of life!" Plaque on wall of Katherine Hepburn's home.

WEDNESDAY 12

Lincoln's Birthday

5:00 Naughton
7:30 Bjerke- *1:30 Dart*

6:15 PM
W. Wright — Pool
647-2121 Ext. 284

 # 26898013

Things may come to those who wait, but only the things left by those who hustle.
— Abraham Lincoln

THURSDAY 13

01330 27302250 -7- 375 1274 *1276*

647-4126

When you reach for the stars, you may not quite get one, but you won't come up with a handful of mud either.
— Leo Burnett

FRIDAY 14

3:00 PM Murphy & Slott

12:45 - 6:15 = 5 1/2 HRS ✓

Review costs & analysis of accounts

He who wants to persuade should put his trust not in the right argument, but in the right word. The power of sound has always been greater than the power of sense.
— Joseph Conrad

SATURDAY 15

SUNDAY 16

(continued from page 20)

Prior to the Twentieth Amendment in this century, we had a "March Barometer" when newly-elected Presidents (Taft, Wilson, Harding, Hoover and Roosevelt) were inaugurated on March 4. Newly-elected Congresses convened in March for the occasion. Score 5 out of 5 for the "March Barometer" prior to the Twentieth Amendment.

Between 1900 and 1933, eight new Congresses convened on the first Monday in December (13 months after the election). But because of annual year-end reinvestment, it would be misleading to use December as a barometer. I used a "November Barometer" instead and the score was almost perfect. In 1903, the only time Congress actually convened in November, the barometer was in error. The Panic of 1903 took the Dow down 37.7% and the new Congress was called in one month earlier, ostensibly to "stem the tide." The Panic ended on November 9, the day Congress convened, but the month remained negative while the market moved up over the next 11 months.

Three other new Congresses were convened in other months for different reasons—April in 1911 and 1917 and May in 1919. The record is a double bulls-eye for the "April Barometer." As for the one-shot "May Barometer" a post-Armistice 30.9% surge in four months (February to May) took May up 13.6% but the 12-month period (including May) almost lost it all. President Wilson spent six months trying to win the peace.

Rather impressive this "New Congress Barometer" which has become the January Barometer since the passage of the Twentieth Amendment.

New Congress Barometers (Odd Years)
NEWLY ELECTED PRESIDENT INAUGURATED MARCH 4TH

March %Change	12 Month's %Change	Same	Opposite
5.2%	11.6%	1909	
0.7	2.4	1913	
1.0	14.0	1921	
-2.7	-14.6	1929	
7.8	101.3	1933	

12 month's % change includes March

NEW CONGRESS CONVENES FIRST WEEK IN DECEMBER 13 MONTHS AFTER ELECTION

November %Change	12 Month's %Change	Same	Opposite
0.9%	2.5%	1901	
-1.8	39.7		1903*
7.3	10.9	1905	
1.2	4.3	1907	
0.7	8.9	1915	
4.3	17.5	1923	
3.5	3.9	1925	
9.1	38.8	1927	
-11.0	-41.3	1931	

*Panic of 1903 ends 11/9 as Congress convenes (off 37.7%)
12 month's % change includes November

NEW CONGRESS CONVENES IN APRIL OR MAY EARLIER THAN USUAL, NO CHANGE IN PRESIDENCY

Month's %Change	12 Month's %Change	Same	Opposite
0.5%	6.0%	1911	
-2.3	-19.6	1917	
13.6	0.7	1919**	

**Wilson in Europe 6 months; Post Armistice surge (up 30.9% Feb to May)
Based on Dow Jones industrial average (1901-1933)
12 month's % change includes applicable month

22

FEBRUARY

MONDAY

17

President's Day
(Market Closed)

YWBHA

I have brought myself, by long meditation,
to the conviction that a human being with a
settled purpose must accomplish it, and that
nothing can resist a will which will stake
even existence upon its fulfillment.
— Benjamin Disraeli

TUESDAY

18

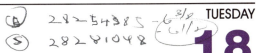

B 282 54385
S 282 81048

Great works are performed not by
strength, but perseverance.
— Samuel Johnson

WEDNESDAY

19

8:30

You've got to think about ''big things''
while you're doing small things, so that
all the small things go
in the right direction.
— Alvin Toffler

THURSDAY

20

1:00ᴾᴹ W. Kelley

R: Slota 4:00PM

Obstacles are those frightful things you
see when you take your eyes off the goal.
— Hannah More

FRIDAY

21

If goal of 8½ is not acheived by
12:45AM Sell at the market

YOEX BP   300 (1)   6½

There have been three great inventions
since the beginning of time. The fire, the
wheel, and central banking.
— Will Rogers

SATURDAY

22

1-800-435-4000

SUNDAY

23

THE SECOND YEAR OF DECADES

Except for 1932 and 1962, "second" years have tended to be gainers though mostly of modest proportions. Republican presidential victories of 1952 and 1972 triggered dynamic market moves in contrast to the Democratic takeovers of 1912 and 1932. The best year was 1922. Next, were 1972 and 1982.

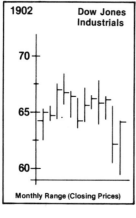

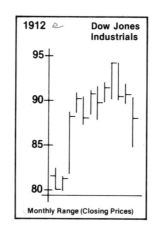

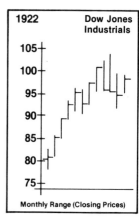

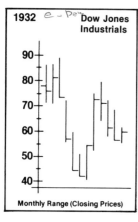

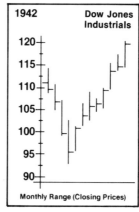

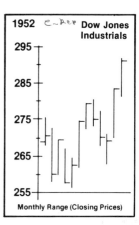

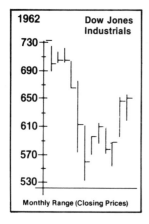

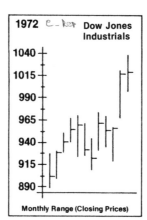

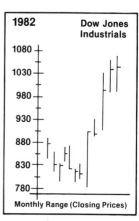

MONDAY

24

I measure what's going on, and I adapt to it. I try to get my ego out of the way. The market is smarter than I am so I bend.
— Martin Zweig

Ident-O-Ring Service
1-800-523-0552

TUESDAY

25

The state is inefficient, the state is corrupt, the state is incompetent and the state is gigantic.
— Fernando Collor de Mello, President of Brazil

Dentene

WEDNESDAY

26

We go to the movies to be entertained, not see rape, ransacking, pillage and looting, we can get all that in the stock market.
— Kennedy Gammage

11:00 PM - J. Goff

Democracon - Afternoon

5:00 PM - P. Miller

VWRHA - Payroll Update and

THURSDAY

27

Liberals have practiced tax and tax, spend and spend, elect and elect but conservatives have perfected borrow and borrow, spend and spend, elect and elect.
— George Will, *Newsweek*, 1989

Pay Keystone Inc. & Cream Bros.

FRIDAY

28

The worst mistake investors make is taking their profits too soon, and their losses too long.
— Michael Price, Mutual Shares Fund

J. Bozzell. - 11:00 PM

SATURDAY

29

SUNDAY

1

Up, up in March is the Dow's direction in the year before a Presidential election

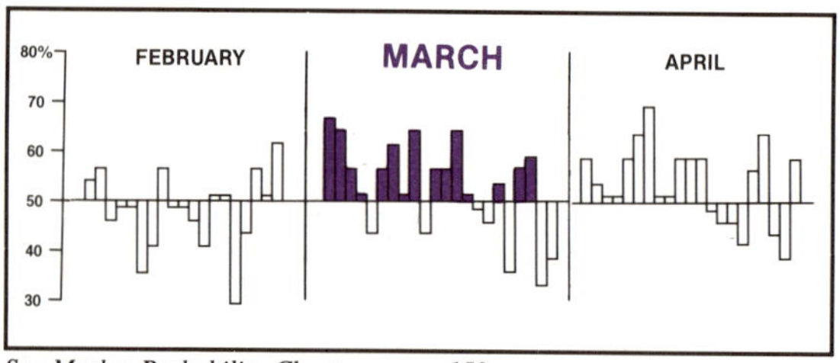

See Market Probability Chart on page 159.

MARCH ALMANAC

MARCH						
S	M	T	W	T	F	S
1	2	3	4	5	6	7
8	9	10	11	12	13	14
15	16	17	18	19	20	21
22	23	24	25	26	27	28
29	30	31				

APRIL						
S	M	T	W	T	F	S
			1	2	3	4
5	6	7	8	9	10	11
12	13	14	15	16	17	18
19	20	21	22	23	24	25
26	27	28	29	30		

☐ "In like a lion, out like a lamb" describes stronger first half than second ☐ Many substantial rallies of at least 5% started here since 1949 ☐ RECORD: S&P 28 up, 14 down ☐ Average S&P gain 1.1%, fifth best ☐ Gain of 451.52 Dow points, third best over 40 years (climbed 109 points in 1986) ☐ Best election month since 1900 as primary season begins.

MARCH DAILY POINT CHANGES DOW JONES INDUSTRIALS

Previous Month Close	1982	1983	1984	1985	1986	1987	1988	1989	1990	1991
	824.39	**1112.62**	**1154.63**	**1284.01**	**1709.06**	**2223.99**	**2071.62**	**2258.39**	**2627.25**	**2882.18**
1	4.00	18.09	4.81	15.35	—	—	−1.16	−15.35	8.34	27.72
2	2.57	4.35	12.04	—	—	−3.52	0.83	22.67	24.77	—
3	−10.66	3.00	—	—	−12.39	6.05	−7.80	8.58	—	—
4	−7.61	2.90	—	−9.83	−10.25	30.93	−5.63	—	—	4.21
5	−0.19	—	−6.28	2.32	0.24	18.98	—	—	−10.81	58.41
6	—	—	−12.67	−11.48	9.94	3.80	—	20.53	27.25	0.75
7	—	0.78	−8.90	−8.84	3.23	—	−1.49	−4.11	−7.21	−9.90
8	−11.89	21.96	3.46	−1.87	—	—	24.70	4.83	26.58	−8.17
9	8.37	12.86	−7.33	—	—	−20.11	−6.80	−4.11	−12.84	—
10	1.05	−11.70	—	—	3.12	19.97	−48.24	−9.29	—	—
11	0.67	−3.20	—	−1.11	43.10	−11.11	8.95	—	—	−15.84
12	−8.19	—	15.60	−3.20	−0.60	−1.64	—	—	3.38	−16.84
13	—	—	9.42	−10.05	8.26	−8.68	—	24.11	−12.16	32.68
14	—	−3.29	1.26	−1.65	39.03	—	15.09	N/C	13.29	−2.97
15	3.62	10.07	1.36	−12.70	—	—	−2.66	14.29	7.88	−3.96
16	2.66	−8.52	16.96	—	—	−10.22	16.91	20.17	45.50	—
17	−2.48	0.97	—	—	−15.92	36.36	21.72	−48.57	—	—
18	9.42	0.77	—	2.32	13.05	2.13	1.33	—	—	−18.32
19	0.38	—	−12.98	21.42	−1.92	12.64	—	—	14.41	−62.13
20	—	—	4.39	−5.85	16.29	33.95	—	−29.64	−16.89	4.21
21	—	7.55	−4.92	2.98	−35.68	—	−20.23	3.75	−10.81	−16.58
22	13.89	−2.32	−14.97	−0.77	—	—	−0.99	−3.04	−32.21	3.46
23	7.13	17.90	−1.04	—	—	30.26	1.49	−20.17	8.56	—
24	−3.33	5.03	—	—	14.37	5.40	−43.77	H	—	—
25	4.29	−5.81	—	−7.51	−4.43	−5.69	−44.92	—	—	6.93
26	−9.71	—	−1.89	−0.22	32.20	9.10	—	—	3.38	49.01
27	—	—	1.36	5.19	11.02	−36.79	—	14.82	29.28	2.72
28	—	−6.77	20.31	−4.20	H	—	0.82	17.68	6.75	−3.71
29	5.90	−2.13	−3.87	6.07	—	—	18.57	5.98	−15.99	H
30	0.67	12.10	−5.86	—	—	−57.39	20.22	−0.18	−20.49	—
31	−1.72	−13.26	—	—	−3.11	26.28	9.94	12.28	—	—
Close	**822.77**	**1130.03**	**1164.89**	**1266.78**	**1818.61**	**2304.69**	**1988.06**	**2293.62**	**2707.21**	**2913.86**
Change	**−1.62**	**17.41**	**10.26**	**−17.23**	**109.55**	**80.70**	**−83.56**	**35.23**	**79.96**	**31.68**

11:00   Hunter

12:00   M.ller

5:00   W. Wright

CHADWICK FUNERAL HOME

CLOSE OUT GENERAL LEDGER

& SET UP CURRENT YEAR   2 1/2 HRS

MONDAY

2

The legal profession has distinguished itself by having 65 of its members indicted in the Watergate scandal.
— Alan Jay Lerner

TUESDAY

3

32620140
32735126

Mac Muller   9:00 PM

Stock prices tend to discount what has been unanimously reported by the mass media.
— Louis Ehrenkrantz

- Ash Wednesday -

WEDNESDAY

4

R. LaPlante   11:00 AM

When prices are high
They want to buy;
When prices are low
They let them go.
— Ian Notley

Dr. Sensone   4:45 PM

THURSDAY

5

It is the growth of total government spending as a percentage of gross national product — not the way it is financed —that crowds out the private sector.
— Paul Craig Roberts, *Business Week*, 1984

FRIDAY

6

NYA	SPX	XMI	OEX	XOC
223.79	404.44	344.44	378.02	480.95
225.36	407.51	346.89	381.08	487.94
223.46	403.65	343.39	377.15	478.71

OR=14995   CR=40157
OQ=44811   CQ=49824
OP=86472   CP=47265
OO=38100   CO=75783

Governments last as long as the under-taxed can defend themselves against the over-taxed.
— Bernard Berenson

CHADWICK FUNERAL HOME

FORMS 1120S & PA   6 HRS ✓

SATURDAY

7

SUNDAY

8

MARKET CHARTS OF ELECTION YEARS

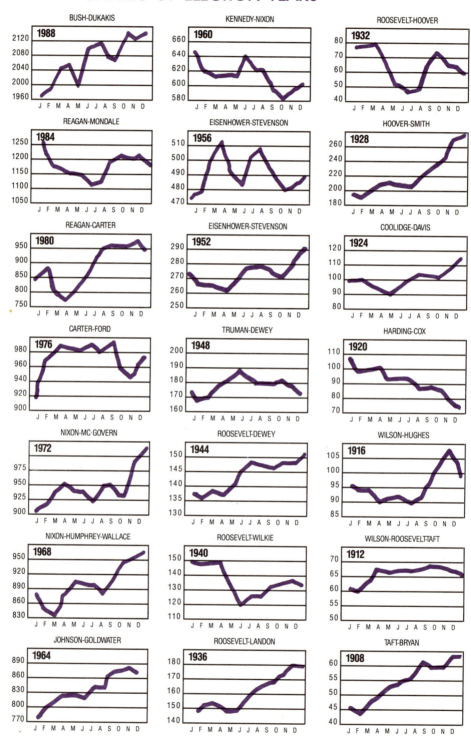

Based on Dow Jones industrial stock average mean of the month

MARCH

MONDAY 9

11:00-12:00 Mrs. Kearns

Always check open interest.
If gap in prices on Mon or Tues sell following
morning - if no gap sell Thurs Morn

TUESDAY 10

2.00 TRACZ
A. Musser - Prepare Form 1120-S

Chadwick Funeral Home
Assemble & Photocopy Tax Return   2 Hrs
Review and deliver - 9X estimated C/S 2 Hrs

WEDNESDAY 11

10:15 - March 11   Dental Appointment
         Dr. Deal - 1001 Loncester Ave
              Bryn Mawr

Murphy & Slota
Analysis of Accounts
Determine differences, etc.   8 HRS ✓

THURSDAY 12

FRIDAY 13

11:00 Mrs. Wilson

SATURDAY 14

SUNDAY 15

PROGNOSTICATING TOOLS AND PATTERNS FOR 1992

For 25 years Almanac readers have profited from being able to predict the timing of the Political Market cycle. To help you gain perspective in 1992, a valuable array of tables, charts and pertinent information can be found on the pages noted:

MARKET CHARTS OF PRESIDENTIAL ELECTION YEARS

Individual charts for each of the century's 22 election years, including candidates and winners. Page 28.

A MAY/JUNE DISASTER LESS LIKELY IN ELECTION YEAR

Politics alters market rhythms quadrennially and favors the last eight months of the year. Page 46.

WINNER OF 1992 ELECTION CAN BE PREDICTED BY DOW'S DIRECTION

A gain between New Year's Day and Election Day tends to precede a victory by the party in power. Page 64.

INCUMBENT VICTORIES VS. INCUMBENT DEFEATS

Graphic presentation shows that markets tend to be stronger when the party in power wins. Page 66.

HOW GOVERNMENT MANIPULATES ECONOMY TO STAY IN POWER

Statistical evidence proves that the money faucets get turned on during years divisible by ''4.'' Page 68.

POST-CONVENTION-TO-ELECTION-DAY FORECASTER

On 15 occasions since 1900 the incumbent party retained power and the market rose 13 times between the last convention and Election Day. Page 74.

MARKET "VOTES" FOR REPUBLICANS IN NOVEMBER

Table shows monthly gain or loss in all election years since 1900 and reveals unusual market patterns in response to political activities. Page 96.

PREDICT 1992 WINNER ONE YEAR IN ADVANCE

Outcome of the 18 elections since 1920 foretold by level of interest rates on November 15 of the preceding year. Page 100.

THE POLITICAL STOCK MARKET CYCLE

Stock prices have been impacted by elections for 159 years, gaining 527% in second half of presidential terms vs. 74% in first half. Page 125.

Additional comment: Unless a domestic debacle (the Depression in 1932) or a foreign debacle (Iran hostage crisis in 1980) occurs, presidents running for re-election to a second term invariably win in a landslide. Gains during such years since 1900 have averaged 8.3%.

MARCH

MONDAY
16

Handwritten: 1:30 Caponi
5:00 (Kraut)

Wall Street has a uniquely hysterical way of thinking the world will end tomorrow but be fully recovered in the long run, then a few years later believing the immediate future is rosy but that the long term stinks.
— Kenneth L. Fisher, *Wall Street Waltz*

St. Patrick's Day
TUESDAY
17

Handwritten: Market should hit low about 12:00 PM

Early in March (1960), Dr. Arthur F. Burns called on me…Burns' conclusion was that unless some decisive action was taken, and taken soon, we were heading for another economic dip which would hit its low point in October, just before the elections. — Richard M. Nixon, *Six Crises*

WEDNESDAY
18

If you can buy all you want of a new issue, you do not want any; if you cannot obtain any, you want all you can buy.
— Rod Fadem
Blunt Ellis Loewi

THURSDAY
19

Make money and the whole nation will conspire to call you a gentleman.
— George Bernard Shaw

FRIDAY

20

Handwritten: 1:00 Bewched

Handwritten: 5:15 - 5:20   KRAMER

Central Bankers are brought up pulling the legs off ants.
— Paul Volker
Quoted by William Grieder
Secrets of the Temple

SATURDAY
21

SUNDAY
22

SPRING PORTFOLIO REVIEW

NO. OF SHARES	SECURITY	A ORIGINAL COST	B CURRENT VALUE	C GAIN (B-A) OR LOSS (A-B)	D % CHANGE (C÷A)	E MONTHS HELD	F CHANGE PER MO. (D÷E)	G ANNUAL RETURN (F×12)
200	Sample Corp.	$10,000	$10,400	$400	4.0%	8	0.5%	6.0%
TOTALS								

Stocks which have achieved their potential

1

2

3

Candidates for addition to portfolio

1

2

3

Stocks which have been disappointments

1

2

3

Investment decisions

1

2

3

R Jones - 12:00 pm

MONDAY

23

The power to tax involves the
power to destroy.
— John Marshall
U S Supreme Court, 1819

TUESDAY

24

The fear of capitalism has compelled
socialism to widen freedom, and the fear
of socialism has compelled capitalism to
increase equality.
— Will and Ariel Durant

WEDNESDAY

25

Nothing contributes so much to
the prosperity and happiness of a
country as high profits.
— David Ricardo
On Protection to Agriculture, 1820

THURSDAY

26

One machine can do the work of fifty
ordinary men. No machine can do
the work of one extraordinary man.
— Elbert Hubbard

Norberth Borough Real Estate Taxes - Pay

FRIDAY

27

The only really smart thing about me
is that I know enough to hire men who
are smarter than I am.
— Charles Walgreen

SATURDAY

28

SUNDAY

29

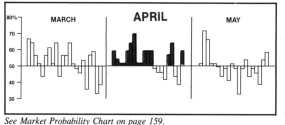

Market does better, two weeks before taxes
Remainder of April, Dow often relaxes

APRIL ALMANAC

APRIL						
S	M	T	W	T	F	S
				1	2	3	4
5	6	7	8	9	10	11
12	13	14	15	16	17	18
19	20	21	22	23	24	25
26	27	28	29	30		

MAY						
S	M	T	W	T	F	S
					1	2
3	4	5	6	7	8	9
10	11	12	13	14	15	16
17	18	19	20	21	22	23
24	25	26	27	28	29	30
31						

See Market Probability Chart on page 159.

☐ More ground is gained in the two weeks prior to the April 15 federal tax deadline than in the last two ☐ When a company's first quarter earnings double, its stock tends to score a 25.2% gain in the previous 30 days and only 5.0% more in the next 30 ☐ RECORD: S&P 28 up, 14 down ☐ Fourth best S&P gain of 1.3% (pg. 38) ☐ Not usually dangerous except in certain sharp bear markets (1962, 1970, 1973, 1974) ☐ Poor record in election years except for two winners caused by exogenous events: Johnson's "withdrawal" in 1968 and Hunt/Silver crisis rebound in 1980.

APRIL DAILY POINT CHANGES DOW JONES INDUSTRIALS

Previous Month	1982	1983	1984	1985	1986	1987	1988	1989	1990	1991
Close	822.77	1130.03	1164.89	1266.78	1818.61	2304.69	1988.06	2293.62	2707.21	2913.86
1	10.47	H	—	5.97	−28.50	11.36	H	—	—	−32.67
2	5.33	—	−11.73	− 7.07	5.15	4.40	—	—	− 6.76	63.86
3	—	—	− 4.40	− 7.62	−28.86	69.89	—	11.18	36.26	−18.32
4	—	− 2.42	− 0.20	0.99	−27.18	—	− 7.46	− 6.60	−17.34	− 2.23
5	− 3.24	− 7.45	−18.01	H	—	—	16.91	6.60	1.80	−27.72
6	4.00	− 6.67	1.67	—	—	15.20	64.16	−12.83	− 4.05	—
7	− 2.48	4.16	—	—	− 3.71	−44.60	0.50	12.83	—	—
8	6.09	7.06	—	− 6.07	34.25	11.22	28.02	—	—	21.78
9	H	—	1.68	0.88	8.86	−32.96	—	—	4.95	−45.54
10	—	—	4.40	6.08	15.68	− 0.42	—	− 2.93	9.01	1.48
11	—	17.12	− 7.33	3.75	− 4.12	—	− 5.80	9.71	− 1.35	30.95
12	− 1.62	3.49	26.17	1.99	—	—	14.09	8.07	22.07	15.34
13	− 0.28	11.32	− 7.01	—	—	−51.71	− 2.98	−23.65	H	—
14	− 2.95	8.61	—	—	15.13	−34.09	−101.46	41.06	—	—
15	1.52	6.09	—	1.10	4.34	29.97	8.29	—	—	12.38
16	3.81	—	10.15	2.77	38.32	− 6.96	—	—	11.26	53.71
17	—	—	4.29	2.76	7.06	H	—	0.73	2.71	17.58
18	—	11.90	− 8.06	− 7.18	−14.63	—	− 5.81	41.61	−32.89	− 5.20
19	2.66	− 8.70	1.57	1.43	—	—	− 8.62	7.51	−20.94	−33.67
20	− 5.52	16.93	H	—	—	− 5.39	−14.09	− 9.53	−15.99	—
21	2.86	− 3.20	—	—	15.50	66.47	− 1.99	32.08	—	—
22	9.70	− 8.03	—	N/C	−24.92	−51.13	27.69	—	—	−37.87
23	9.04	—	− 8.58	12.15	− 1.37	− 4.97	—	—	−29.28	2.73
24	—	—	13.40	− 0.22	2.11	−45.60	—	− 6.78	−12.17	19.05
25	—	− 9.09	0.63	6.29	3.85	—	20.88	−15.77	11.94	−28.46
26	3.42	22.25	11.72	− 9.60	—	—	8.79	2.20	10.14	− 8.66
27	− 8.08	− 1.06	− 6.18	—	—	− 4.83	3.15	29.88	−31.53	—
28	− 4.86	11.12	—	—	8.18	1.42	− 6.63	− 0.19	—	—
29	− 7.70	6.68	—	−15.46	−17.86	22.30	− 8.95	—	—	−35.40
30	3.42	—	1.68	− 1.66	−41.91	32.10	—	—	11.71	10.89
Close	848.36	1226.20	1170.75	1258.06	1783.98	2286.36	2032.33	2418.80	2656.76	2887.87
Change	25.59	96.17	5.86	− 8.72	−34.63	−18.33	44.27	125.18	−50.45	−25.99

34

MAR/APRIL

MONDAY
30

I am first and foremost a catalyst. I bring
people and situations together.
— Armand Hammer

TUESDAY
31

March
W. Davis 11:00 AM

131,200

1) 2 - 3/4
4 0

The average man…is always waiting for
something to happen to him instead of
setting to work to make things happen.
— A.A. Milne

WEDNESDAY
1

YWBHA - Depreciation Schedules - 3 Hrs

It is impossible to please all the world
and one's father.
— Jean de La Fontaine

THURSDAY
2

YWBHA - Worksheet and Annual Report
Preparation   - 12 Hrs

Good judgment is usually the result of
experience and experience frequently
is the result of bad judgment.
— Robert Lovell
Quoted by Robert Sobel,
Panic on Wall Street

FRIDAY
3

YWBHA - Annual Reports   - 3 Hrs

Every human being, no matter how
beaten down, dreams of a better life
and will work like a champion for
it given the opportunity.
— Mildred & Glen Leet
Founders of "Trickle Up"

SATURDAY
4

SUNDAY
5

FIRST HALF OF APRIL
OUTPERFORMS SECOND HALF

Most people believe Uncle Sam has a chilling effect on stock prices in early April. They assume many investors sell some of their holdings to pay income taxes. Once the April 15 tax deadline passes, they assume the market will turn up as tax selling ceases. However, the obvious is seldom true in investing. From 1955 through 1991, the first half of April outperformed the second half 25 out of 37 times. The former gained 1.4% on average compared to a small loss for the latter. April's last two weeks were superior in the last four presidential years.

MARKET PERFORMANCE IN APRIL

	End Of March	Mid-April Tax Deadline	End of April	April 1-15	April 16-30
1955	36.58*	37.96*	37.96*	3.8%	0.0%
1956	48.48	47.96	48.38	—1.1	0.9
1957	44.11	44.95	45.74	1.9	1.8
1958	42.10	42.43	43.44	0.8	2.4
1959	55.44	56.98	57.59	2.8	1.1
1960	55.34	56.59	54.37	2.3	—3.9
1961	65.06	66.68	65.31	2.5	—2.1
1962	69.55	67.60	65.24	—2.8	—3.6
1963	66.57	69.09	69.80	3.8	1.1
1964	78.98	80.09	79.46	1.4	—0.8
1965	86.16	88.15	89.11	2.3	1.1
1966	89.23	91.99	91.06	3.1	—1.0
1967	90.20	91.07	94.01	1.0	3.2
1968	90.20	96.59	97.59	7.1	1.0
1969	101.51	101.53	103.69	0.0	2.1
1970	89.63	86.73	81.52	—3.2	—6.0
1971	100.31	103.52	103.95	3.2	0.4
1972	107.20	109.51	107.67	2.2	—1.7
1973	111.52	111.44	106.97	—0.1	—4.0
1974	93.98	94.36	90.91	0.4	—4.3
1975	83.36	86.30	87.30	3.5	1.2
1976	102.77	100.67	101.64	—2.0	1.0
1977	98.42	101.04	98.44	2.7	—2.6
1978	89.21	94.45	96.83	5.9	2.5
1979	101.59	101.12	101.76	—0.5	0.6
1980	102.09	102.63	106.29	0.5	3.6
1981	136.00	134.70	132.81	—1.0	—1.4
1982	111.96	116.35	116.44	3.9	0.1
1983	152.96	158.75	164.42	3.8	3.6
1984	159.18	158.32	160.05	—0.5	1.1
1985	180.66	180.92	179.83	0.1	—0.6
1986	238.90	237.73	235.52	—0.5	—0.9
1987	291.70	284.44	288.36	—2.5	1.4
1988	258.89	259.77	261.33	0.3	0.8
1989	294.87	301.72	309.64	2.3	2.6
1990	339.94	344.74	330.80	1.4	—4.1
1991	375.22	381.19	375.35	1.6	—1.5

*S & P Composite Index   **Average**   **1.4%**   **—0.1%**

Five of the ten Aprils with no market gains in the first half of the month were in bear market years. However, these declining years had more of an adverse effect on the last two weeks of the month. The table begins with 1955, as March 15 was the income tax deadline in prior years. When April 15 falls on the weekend and the IRS extends its deadline, the following Monday's market average is used.

APRIL

MONDAY 6

9:30 Dr. Unzengst

YWBHA Reports 6 Hrs

> Only buy stocks when the market declines
> 10% from that date a year ago, which
> happens once or twice a decade.
> — Eugene D. Brody
> Oppenheimer Capital

TUESDAY 7

2:00 PM Dr. Varengst

> Sell stocks whenever the market
> is 30% higher over a year ago.
> — Eugene D. Brody
> Oppenheimer Capital

WEDNESDAY 8

Stuart, M. & M   5:00 PM

> You have to figure out how the consensus
> is wrong to be valuable to the client.
> — Edward Yardeni
> Prudential Bache

THURSDAY 9

Buy Calls - Intel in morning

> Never will a man penetrate deeper into
> error than when he is continuing on a road
> that has led him to great success.
> — Friedrich von Hayek
> Counterrevolution of Science

FRIDAY 10

Pay Narberth Real Estate Taxs

> Never overpay for a stock. More money
> is lost than in any other way by projecting
> above-average growth and paying
> an extra multiple for it.
> — Charles Neuhauser
> Bear, Stearns

4:00 Olson -

SATURDAY 11

11:30 A.M. Kawano

SUNDAY 12

BEST MONTHS IN PAST 41⅓ YEARS

Seasonality for different months of the year is usually based on the number of times the month has closed higher in either the Dow industrials or the S&P 500. A much more dramatic picture is presented when percent changes are cumulated.

November ranks Number One with an average monthly gain of 1.7% since 1950 based on the S&P 500. Next comes December 1.6%, January 1.6%, April 1.3%, March 1.1% and July 1.1%. Using Dow points as a measuring stick is misleading as the Dow was mostly under 1000 prior to 1982. The worst two months are: September, down 482.99 on the Dow and 26.9% on the S&P; and May, up one, down the other.

MONTHLY % AND POINT CHANGES (JANUARY 1950-APRIL 1991)

Standard & Poor's 500					Dow Jones Industrials				
Month	Total % Change	Avg. % Change	# Up	# Dn	Month	Total Points Change	Avg. Points Change	# Up	# Dn
Jan	65.1	1.6	26	16	Jan	678.76	16.16	28	14
Feb	3.3	0.1	22	20	Feb	258.24	6.15	23	19
Mar	47.7	1.1	28	14	Mar	451.52	10.75	27	15
Apr	52.6	1.3	28	14	Apr	504.05	12.00	26	16
May	− 4.1	−0.1	21	20	May	50.25	1.23	19	22
Jun	10.7	0.3	21	20	Jun	163.03	3.98	21	20
Jul	45.1	1.1	23	18	Jul	377.04	9.20	24	17
Aug	11.1	0.3	22	19	Aug	42.50	1.04	23	18
Sep	−26.9	−0.7	17	24	Sep	−482.99	−11.78	14	27
Oct	15.5	0.4	22	19	Oct	−413.04	−10.07	22	19
Nov	67.8	1.7	27	14	Nov	407.96	9.95	27	14
Dec	65.2	1.6	30	11	Dec	650.72	15.87	29	12

% Rank					Points Rank				
Nov	67.8	1.7	27	14	Jan	678.76	16.16	28	14
Dec	65.2	1.6	30	11	Dec	650.72	15.87	29	12
Jan	65.1	1.6	26	16	Apr	504.05	12.00	26	16
Apr	52.6	1.3	28	14	Mar	451.52	10.75	27	15
Mar	47.7	1.1	28	14	Nov	407.96	9.95	27	14
Jul	45.1	1.1	23	18	Jul	377.04	9.20	24	17
Oct	15.5	0.4	22	19	Feb	258.24	6.15	23	19
Aug	11.1	0.3	22	19	Jun	163.03	3.98	21	20
Jun	10.7	0.3	21	20	May	50.25	1.23	19	22
Feb	3.3	0.1	22	20	Aug	42.50	1.04	23	18
May	−4.1	−0.1	21	20	Oct	−413.04	−10.07	22	19
Sep	−26.9	−0.7	17	24	Sep	−482.99	−11.78	14	27

The crash of 1987 with its massive move in Dow points severely affected the Dow point ranking. October (down 602.75) fell to last position from sixth the year before and November (down 159.98) dropped from second place to sixth. The effect was less noticeable when measured percentage-wise.

APRIL

MONDAY
13

I invest in people, not ideas; I want to see
fire in the belly *and* intellect.
— Arthur Rock

TUESDAY
14

Unless you've interpreted changes
before they've occurred, you'll be
decimated trying to follow them.
— Robert J. Nurock

WEDNESDAY
15

There's nothing wrong with cash.
It gives you time to think.
— Robert Prechter, Jr.,
Elliott Wave Theorist

THURSDAY
 # 16

The big guys are the status quo,
not the innovators.
— Kenneth L. Fisher

Good Friday (Market Closed)   ## FRIDAY
17

A bull market tends to bail you out of all
your mistakes. Conversely, bear markets
make you PAY for your mistakes.
— Richard Russell

Passover   ## SATURDAY
18

Easter   ## SUNDAY
19

DOW GAINS 2937.05 NOVEMBER THROUGH APRIL IN 41 YEARS LOSES 263.21 MAY THROUGH OCTOBER

To have invested in the market between November First and April Thirtieth each year, and to have switched into fixed income securities for the other six months of the year, back and forth, would have been an excellent strategy during the second half of this century. A glance at the "Best Months" table on page 38, or the chart on page 121, shows that November, December, January, March and April have been the top five months of the year since 1950. Add February, and a new strategy is born. These six consecutive months gained 2937.05 points for the Dow industrials in 41 years, while the remaining six May through October months were losing 263.21 points.

Percentage changes in the Standard & Poor's composite index for each six-month segment since 1950 are shown alongside a compounding $10,000 investment. May/October's puny $3,177 gain is completely overshadowed by November/April's $147,002. Just two November/April's losses were double-digited and were due to exogenous factors: our April 1970 Cambodian invasion and the fall 1973 OPEC oil embargo.

Don't tell the big boys about this! Let's keep this one to ourselves.

SIX-MONTH SWITCHING STRATEGY

Year	S & P % Change May 1 Through Oct.31	Investing $10,000	S & P % Change Nov. 1 Through Apr.30	Investing $10,000
1950	8.1%	10,810	14.8%	$ 11,480
1951	2.3	11,059	1.7	11,675
1952	5.1	11,623	0.4	11,722
1953	− 0.3	11,588	19.8	14,043
1954	12.5	13,036	14.8	16,121
1955	11.5	14,535	14.3	18,426
1956	− 5.8	13,692	0.4	18,500
1957	−10.2	12,296	5.8	19,573
1958	18.2	14,534	12.2	21,961
1959	− 0.1	14,519	− 5.5	20,753
1960	− 1.8	14,258	22.3	25,381
1961	5.1	14,985	− 4.9	24,138
1962	−13.4	12,977	23.5	29,810
1963	6.0	13,755	7.4	32,016
1964	6.8	14,691	5.0	33,617
1965	3.7	15,234	− 1.5	33,112
1966	−11.9	13,421	17.2	38,808
1967	− 0.1	13,287	3.9	40,321
1968	6.0	14,085	0.3	40,442
1969	− 6.2	13,211	−16.2	33,890
1970	2.1	13,489	24.9	42,329
1971	− 9.4	12,221	14.3	48,382
1972	3.6	12,661	− 4.1	46,399
1973	1.2	12,929	−16.6	38,696
1974	−18.2	10,576	18.1	45,700
1975	2.0	10,788	14.2	52,190
1976	1.2	10,917	− 4.3	49,946
1977	− 6.2	10,240	4.9	52,393
1978	− 3.8	9,851	9.2	57,213
1979	0.1	9,861	4.4	59,730
1980	19.9	11,823	4.2	62,239
1981	− 8.3	10,842	− 4.5	59,439
1982	14.8	12,446	23.0	73,109
1983	− 0.5	12,384	− 2.1	71,574
1984	3.8	12,855	8.2	77,443
1985	5.6	13,575	24.0	96,030
1986	3.6	14,063	18.2	113,507
1987	−12.7	12,277	3.8	117,820
1988	6.8	13,112	11.0	130,789
1989	9.4	14,339	− 2.8	127,127
1990	− 8.1	13,177	23.5	157,002
41-Year Gain		**$ 3,177**		**$147,002**

APRIL

MONDAY 20

CPA License Application
~.21

> To turn $100 into $110 is work. To turn
> $100 million into $110 million
> is inevitable.
> — Edgar Bronfman, Seagrams
> in *Newsweek*, 1985

TUESDAY 21

> Almost any insider purchase is worth
> investigating for a possible lead to a
> superior speculation. But very few
> insider sales justify concern.
> — William Chidester

WEDNESDAY 22

Coles House — 1st Qtr. Payroll Taxes - Review
15.21 — Report review

> If the models are telling you to sell,
> sell, sell, but only buyers are out
> there, don't be a jerk. Buy!
> — William Silber, Ph.D. (N.Y.U.)
> in *Newsweek*, 1986

THURSDAY 23

15.30

> The higher a people's intelligence and
> moral strength, the lower will be
> the prevailing rate of interest.
> — Eugen von Bohm-Bawerk, 1910

FRIDAY 24

15.25

> When everybody starts looking really
> smart, and not realizing that a lot of it
> was luck, I get scared.
> — Raphael Yavneh, Forbes

SATURDAY 25

SUNDAY 26

WARNING: MAY AND JUNE MIGHT BE HAZARDOUS TO YOUR WEALTH

Not once in the ten years 1965-1974 was the Dow Jones industrial average able to chalk up a net gain between May 1 and June 30. Then came 1975, and the May-June market curse was finally crushed. However, it took the greatest half-year gain in history (265.75 Dow points) to break the spell.

While June was the weakest market month since the early fifties, May was getting clobbered with monotonous regularity up until recent years. As a result, May had conquered last place in the performance derby. In the last 27 years, the market in May, as measured by the Dow, lost ground 17 out of 27 times, in contrast to the 1955-1964 period when May was a loser only thrice.

The figures below show an average 0.6% deline for May since 1965. June also was a loser until recent years. Peering down the performance columns of the two months, you can see that, in most years, if one month didn't get you the other did (1975, 1980, 1985, 1986, 1987 and 1990 were exceptions.)

The most logical reason for weak Mays in the past was that the market tended to rise sharply in bull years through the first quarter and into April, becoming overextended in May. In bear years, declines started slowly and picked up steam in May and June.

Seven generally fat years produced seven straight gains during recent May-June periods. What happened to May-June disasters? I notice the Dow has declined in five of the seven last Aprils. It's possible we're experiencing a seasonality shift.

THE MAY-JUNE DISASTER AREA

	End of Month Dow Jones Industrials			Net % Change		Both
	April	May	June	May	June	Months
1965	922.31	918.04	868.03	— 0.5%	— 5.4%	— 5.9%
1966	933.68	884.07	870.10	— 5.3	— 1.6	— 6.8
1967	897.05	852.56	860.26	— 5.0	0.9	— 4.1
1968	912.22	899.00	897.80	— 1.4	— 0.1	— 1.6
1969	950.18	937.56	873.19	— 1.3	— 6.9	— 8.1
1970	736.07	700.44	683.53	— 4.8	— 2.4	— 7.1
1971	941.75	907.81	891.14	— 3.6	— 1.8	— 5.4
1972	954.17	960.72	929.03	0.7	— 3.3	— 2.6
1973	921.43	901.41	891.71	— 2.2	— 1.1	— 3.2
1974	836.75	802.17	802.41	— 4.1	0.0	— 4.1
1975	821.34	832.29	878.99	1.3	5.6	7.0
1976	996.85	975.23	1002.78	— 2.2	2.8	0.6
1977	926.90	898.66	916.30	— 3.0	2.0	— 1.1
1978	837.32	840.61	818.95	0.4	— 2.6	— 2.2
1979	854.90	822.33	841.98	— 3.8	2.4	— 1.5
1980	817.06	850.85	867.92	4.1	2.0	6.2
1981	997.75	991.75	976.88	— 0.6	— 1.5	— 2.1
1982	848.36	819.54	811.93	— 3.4	— 0.9	— 4.3
1983	1226.20	1199.98	1221.96	— 2.1	1.8	— 0.3
1984	1170.75	1104.85	1132.40	— 5.6	2.5	— 3.3
1985	1258.06	1315.41	1335.46	4.6	1.5	6.2
1986	1783.98	1876.71	1892.72	5.2	0.9	6.1
1987	2286.36	2291.57	2418.53	0.2	5.5	5.8
1988	2032.33	2031.12	2141.71	— 0.1	5.4	5.4
1989	2418.80	2480.15	2440.06	2.5	— 1.6	0.9
1990	2656.76	2876.66	2880.69	8.3	0.1	8.4
1991	2887.87	3027.50	2906.75	4.8	— 4.0	0.7
			Average change	— 0.6	0.0	— 0.6

VW NFX   VWNDX

MONDAY
27

15.21

TUESDAY
28

15.06   12.24

WEDNESDAY
29

A 715   D 959   U 567   H 30   L 29
15.13   12.34

THURSDAY
30

A 1092   D 606   U 6
Call Anna Grundy Fisher
15.17   12.39

FRIDAY
1

L. CHADWICK - INHERITANCE TAX
MURPHY o SLOTA - 4 HR. ✓

COST WRITE OFFS

REVIEW - PARTNERSHIP LOAN A10

15.12   12.31

SATURDAY
2

SUNDAY
3

In the very merry month of May
Bullish schemes gang aft agley

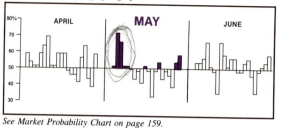

MAY ALMANAC

See Market Probability Chart on page 159.

	MAY					
S	M	T	W	T	F	S
					1	2
3	4	5	6	7	8	9
10	11	12	13	14	15	16
17	18	19	20	21	22	23
24	25	26	27	28	29	30
31						

	JUNE					
S	M	T	W	T	F	S
	1	2	3	4	5	6
7	8	9	10	11	12	13
14	15	16	17	18	19	20
21	22	23	24	25	26	27
28	29	30				

□ May markets tend to come in like bulls, exit like bears □ Airlines have often hit seasonal highs in May □ May is a "disaster" month and most "hazardous to one's wealth" (1985 through 1991 Mays were exceptions) □ RECORD: S&P up 10, down 5, 1950-64; up 11, down 15, 1965-90 □ Second worst month in S&P 500, off 0.1% on average; Dow down 50.25 points since 1950 □ Good election-year month since 1950 up 6, down 3 □ Two big losers were in "re-election" years (1956, 1984).

MAY DAILY POINT CHANGES DOW JONES INDUSTRIALS

Previous Month Close	1981	1982	1983	1984	1985	1986	1987	1988	1989	1990
	997.75	848.36	1226.20	1170.75	1258.06	1783.98	2286.36	2032.33	2418.80	2656.76
1	− 2.16	—	—	12.25	−16.01	− 6.20	− 5.96	—	− 3.84	12.16
2	—	—	−21.87	3.56	0.22	− 3.10	—	10.94	−12.10	20.72
3	—	0.67	3.68	− 5.03	4.97	—	—	15.09	− 9.16	6.53
4	−16.48	5.42	4.64	−16.22	—	—	5.82	−22.05	− 8.80	14.19
5	− 6.67	N/C	7.07	—	—	19.09	51.85	−16.08	− 2.94	—
6	0.90	8.75	12.87	—	0.55	− 5.82	4.12	−12.77	—	—
7	5.05	6.00	—	1.25	−12.65	− 7.53	—	—	—	11.26
8	− 1.99	—	—	9.74	− 2.98	10.91	−12.36	—	− 5.49	11.94
9	—	—	− 4.36	−10.78	10.49	3.22	—	−10.11	− 5.14	− 0.68
10	—	− 8.28	1.45	1.67	13.91	—	—	6.30	3.12	5.63
11	−12.96	4.95	− 9.96	−10.05	—	—	−15.00	−37.80	8.43	63.07
12	7.38	− 0.10	− 5.32	—	—	− 2.10	15.30	2.15	56.82	—
13	− 3.06	− 6.66	4.35	—	3.32	− 1.99	7.08	22.55	—	—
14	5.31	− 1.33	—	− 6.07	− 4.20	22.94	− 4.19	—	—	19.95
15	12.88	—	—	− 0.21	0.22	33.60	−52.97	—	24.19	0.92
16	—	—	−15.77	2.30	4.53	14.88	—	17.08	−10.44	− 2.77
17	—	−12.46	2.81	−10.89	7.29	—	—	−21.22	8.98	12.03
18	− 0.18	− 4.47	− 2.23	− 8.48	—	—	−13.86	−35.32	7.69	−11.80
19	− 5.76	− 4.95	−12.19	—	—	− 1.62	−37.38	7.63	30.98	—
20	− 3.15	− 3.42	− 1.35	—	19.54	25.80	− 5.41	− 6.13	—	—
21	− 0.27	3.42	—	− 8.48	4.82	− 8.81	9.90	—	—	24.77
22	− 4.87	—	—	− 8.69	− 5.94	31.13	17.43	—	0.92	7.55
23	—	—	10.54	− 2.82	− 7.05	16.99	—	−11.11	−24.01	4.03
24	—	0.48	18.48	−10.37	5.26	—	—	21.05	5.86	− 0.71
25	H	− 1.81	9.97	3.67	—	—	H	− 1.16	− 1.28	−34.63
26	12.24	− 5.80	− 5.52	—	—	H	54.74	5.38	11.18	—
27	9.18	− 3.81	− 7.35	—	H	29.74	− 2.13	−10.31	—	—
28	1.11	− 5.42	—	H	− 0.45	25.25	14.87	—	—	H
29	− 2.50	—	—	− 5.86	1.46	4.07	−19.11	—	H	49.57
30	—	—	H	1.35	2.80	− 5.64	—	H	−18.22	8.07
31	—	H	−16.16	2.26	9.63	—	—	74.68	4.60	− 1.90
Close	991.75	819.54	1199.98	1104.85	1315.41	1876.71	2291.57	2031.12	2480.15	2876.66
Change	− 6.00	−28.82	−26.22	−65.90	57.35	92.73	5.21	− 1.21	61.35	219.90

MAY

MONDAY 4

Murphy & Slote   6 Hrs ✓

Adjust for differences

Account analysis

15.30   12.41

TUESDAY 5

Murphy & Slote.

11:00 Am to 7:00 PM = 8 HRS ✓

Review differences + analysis

15.33   12.47

21.33
15.14

WEDNESDAY 6

L. CHADWICK — CHADWICK FUNERAL HOME

15.35   12.52

THURSDAY 7

CHADWICK FUNERAL HOME   10:00AM

L.M. Meve. & B.P. Tax   1½ Hrs ✓

Computer Instr. & reconciling

differences for the months

of Jan. & Feb. — 1992   3 Hrs ✓

FRIDAY 8

Mrs. Fisher   12:00 AM.

SATURDAY 9

SUNDAY 10

Mother's Day

A MAY/JUNE DISASTER LEAST LIKELY IN PRESIDENTIAL YEAR

Election years are traditionally up-years because incumbent administrations shamelessly try to massage the economy so voters will press the right levers in November and keep them in power. Sometimes, overpowering events take precedence and the market crumbles, usually resulting in a change of political control: The Republicans won in 1920 as the post-war economy contracted and President Wilson ailed; the Democrats came back during the 1932 Depression when the Dow hit its lowest level of the century; a world at war and the fall of France jolted the market in 1940, but Roosevelt won an unprecedented third term. Since then, investors have barely been bruised during election years, except for a brief span. In the table below, a very positive picture can be seen for May and June and especially the last eight months of the year:

• January through April losses occurred in four of the ten previous election years. Ironically, bear markets began in the year following each of five gainers while the bear market following the 1964 election was delayed 12 months by the Vietnam acceleration.

• Only three of the last ten presidential Mays were down, in 1956, 1972, and 1984. During two of the years, the market was in the process of topping out.

• Only one June (1972) in the presidential series was a loser. The market moved higher in the others.

• Comparing month-end June with month-end April shows losses only in 1956, 1972, and 1984, for the sixty-day period.

• Looking at the ten Julys in the cycle, five were losers (1960, 1968, 1976, 1984, and 1988). Four were years when at convention time no strong incumbent was running for reelection, which created a climate of uncertainty. Note that April through July periods had only two losers: In 1972, and by a small margin at that, and in 1984, as the market was turning around.

• For a longer perspective, we've extended the table out to December and see only one losing eight-month period in an election year between April and December of 3.5% in 1956. The other years had gains of 4.5 to 27.7%.

LAST EIGHT MONTHS OF ELECTION YEARS BULLISH

Election Year	Change First Four Months	Monthly Closings, Standard & Poor's Composite index					April to Dec.
		April	May	June	July	December	
1952	—1.9	23.32	23.86	24.96	25.40	26.57	13.9%
1956	6.4	48.38	**45.20**	46.97	49.39	46.67	—3.5
1960	—9.2	54.37	55.83	56.92	**55.51**	58.11	6.9
1964	5.9	79.46	80.97	81.69	83.18	84.75	6.7
1968	1.2	97.59	98.68	99.58	**97.74**	103.86	6.4
1972	5.3	107.67	109.53	**107.14**	107.39	118.05	9.6
1976	12.7	101.64	**100.18**	104.28	**103.24**	107.46	5.7
1980	—0.9	106.29	111.24	114.24	121.67	135.76	27.7
1984	—3.0	160.05	**150.55**	153.18	**150.66**	167.24	4.5
1988	5.8	261.33	262.16	273.50	**272.02**	277.72	6.3

* Down months are **bold**.

MONDAY

11

15.39   12.59

The market is a voting machine, whereon
countless individuals register choices
which are the product partly of
reason and partly of emotion.
— Graham & Dodd

TUESDAY

12

Murphy & Slote — Form 1065 —

Summary & worksheet   ~6 hours ✓

Intensd & Review   ~1 hour ✓

with ✓

15.32   12.55   Worksheet   2 hours

Your emotions are often a reverse
indicator of what you ought to be doing.
— John F. Hindelong, Dillon, Reed

WEDNESDAY

13

L. Chadwick Estate

Telephone conferences with RAC in ②
reference to Inheritance Tax & Administration
Form SS-4   — 1½ Hrs

15.38   12.57

Previous review of Grantor Trust   1½ Hrs

When the S&P Index Future premium
over "Cash" gets too high, I sell the
future and buy the stocks. If the
premium disappears, well, buy the future
and sell the stocks.
— Neil Elliott, Fahnestock

THURSDAY

14

15.28   12.50

To me, the "tape" is the final arbiter
of any investment decision. I have
a cardinal rule: Never fight the tape!
— Martin Zweig

FRIDAY

☠ # 15

Stocks are super attractive when the Fed
is loosening and interest rates are falling.
In sum: Don't fight the Fed!
— Martin Zweig

SATURDAY

16

SUNDAY

17

DON'T SELL STOCKS ON MONDAY

I computed the Dow's performance for different days of the week for each year since 1953 and summarized the results below. The most shocking revelation is the Monday "horror show." While the market during 38 years was gaining 2341 Dow points, Mondays alone were losing an astounding 1897 points. Until 1975, Mondays were losers on balance every year except for the big bull years of 1954 and 1958, and 1968 (market closed Wednesdays last seven months). While Wednesdays gained most points, Fridays were up much more often. An army of S&P 500 traders must be causing recent bad Thursdays.

ANNUAL DOW POINT CHANGES FOR DAYS OF THE WEEK SINCE 1953

Year	Monday	Tuesday	Wednesday	Thursday	Friday	Year's Closing D.J.I.	Year's Point Change
1953	− 37.39	− 6.70	19.63	7.25	6.21	280.90	− 11.00
1954	9.81	9.14	24.31	36.05	44.18	404.39	123.49
1955	− 56.09	34.31	45.83	1.18	58.78	488.40	84.01
1956	− 30.15	− 16.36	− 15.30	9.86	63.02	499.47	11.07
1957	−111.28	− 5.93	64.12	4.26	− 14.95	435.69	− 63.78
1958	14.36	26.73	29.10	24.25	53.52	583.65	147.96
1959	− 35.69	20.25	4.11	19.98	87.06	679.36	95.71
1960	−104.89	− 9.90	− 5.62	10.36	46.58	615.89	− 63.47
1961	− 17.76	4.29	67.51	14.26	46.95	731.14	115.25
1962	− 88.44	13.03	9.97	− 4.46	− 9.14	652.10	− 79.04
1963	− 43.61	81.85	16.23	26.07	30.31	762.95	110.85
1964	− 3.70	− 14.53	39.84	21.96	67.61	874.13	111.18
1965	− 70.23	36.65	57.03	2.75	68.93	969.26	95.13
1966	−126.23	− 54.74	56.13	− 45.69	− 13.04	785.69	−183.57
1967	− 73.07	35.93	25.41	98.37	32.78	905.11	119.42
1968*	3.38	37.97	25.16	− 59.00	31.13	943.75	38.64
1969	−152.05	− 48.82	18.33	17.79	21.36	800.36	−143.39
1970	− 99.00	− 47.14	116.07	1.81	66.82	838.92	38.56
1971	− 16.16	22.46	13.66	6.25	25.07	890.20	51.28
1972	− 85.08	− 3.55	65.24	16.14	137.07	1020.02	129.82
1973	−192.68	29.09	− 5.94	41.56	− 41.19	850.86	−169.16
1974	−131.00	29.11	− 20.28	− 12.60	− 99.85	616.24	−234.62
1975	59.74	−129.96	56.75	129.66	119.98	852.41	236.17
1976	81.16	61.32	50.89	− 26.80	− 14.33	1004.65	152.24
1977	− 66.38	− 43.60	− 79.70	− 2.74	18.94	831.17	−173.48
1978	− 31.81	− 70.32	71.33	− 65.71	70.35	805.01	− 26.16
1979	− 27.82	4.72	− 18.84	73.97	1.70	838.74	33.73
1980	− 89.40	138.02	137.67	−112.78	51.74	963.99	125.25
1981	− 64.47	− 30.72	− 13.95	− 13.66	33.81	875.00	− 88.99
1982	21.69	70.22	28.27	14.75	36.61	1046.54	171.54
1983	39.34	− 39.75	149.68	47.90	14.93	1258.64	212.10
1984	− 40.48	44.70	−139.24	94.36	− 6.41	1211.57	− 47.07
1985	87.06	46.00	51.26	56.05	94.73	1546.67	335.10
1986	− 56.03	113.72	178.65	32.17	80.77	1895.95	349.28
1987	−651.77	328.45	392.03	142.47	−168.30	1938.83	42.88
1988	139.28	295.28	− 60.48	−220.90	76.56	2168.57	229.74
1989	− 3.23	93.25	233.25	70.08	191.28	2753.20	584.63
1990	153.11	41.57	47.90	−330.48	− 31.64	2633.66	−119.54
Totals	**−1896.96**	**1096.04**	**1736.01**	**126.74**	**1279.93**		**2341.76**

* Most Wednesdays closed last 7 mos.

MONDAY

18

Every successful enterprise requires
three people — a dreamer, a businessman,
and a son-of-a-bitch.
— Peter McArthur, 1904

TUESDAY

19

The public may boo me, but when I go
home and think of my money, I clap.
— Horace, *Epistles*, c. 20 B.C.

WEDNESDAY

20

Short Interest
Meltdown will occur after
2 month drop in short Interest

Keep away from people who try to
belittle your ambitions. Small people
always do that, but the really great
make you feel that you, too,
can become great.
— Mark Twain

THURSDAY

21

Edison has done more toward
abolishing poverty than all the
reformers and statesmen.
— Henry Ford

FRIDAY

22

15.31

I always keep these seasonal patterns in
the back of my mind. My antennae start
to purr at certain times of the year.
— Kenneth Ward

SATURDAY

23

SUNDAY

24

1990 DAILY DOW POINT CHANGES
(Dow Jones Industrial Average)

WEEK #	MONDAY	TUESDAY	WEDNESDAY	THURSDAY	FRIDAY	WEEKLY DOW CLOSE	NET POINT CHANGE
					1989 Close	2753.20	
1	H	56.95	— 0.42	—13.65	—22.83	2773.25	20.05
2	21.12	—28.37	—15.36	10.03	—71.46	2689.21	— 84.04
3	—19.84	23.25	—33.49	7.25	11.52	2677.90	— 11.31
4	—77.45	14.87	—10.88	—43.46	— 1.75	2559.23	—118.67
5	— 5.85	—10.14	47.30	— 4.28	16.44	2602.70	43.47
6	19.82	—16.21	33.78	4.28	3.83	2648.20	45.50
7	—29.06	4.96	0.22	25.23	—13.96	2635.59	— 12.61
8	H	—38.74	—13.29	— 8.79	—10.58	2564.19	— 71.40
9	38.29	14.64	10.13	8.34	24.77	2660.36	96.17
10	—10.81	27.25	— 7.21	26.58	—12.84	2683.33	22.97
11	3.38	—12.16	13.29	7.88	45.50	2741.22	57.89
12	14.41	—16.89	—10.81	—32.21	8.56	2704.28	— 36.94
13	3.38	29.28	6.75	—15.99	—20.49	2707.21	2.93
14	— 6.76	36.26	—17.34	1.80	— 4.05	2717.12	9.91
15	4.95	9.01	— 1.35	22.07	H	2751.80	34.68
16	11.26	2.71	—32.89	—20.94	—15.99	2695.95	— 55.85
17	—29.28	—12.17	11.94	10.14	—31.53	2645.05	— 50.90
18	11.71	12.16	20.72	6.53	14.19	2710.36	65.31
19	11.26	11.94	— 0.68	5.63	63.07	2801.58	91.22
20	19.95	0.92	— 2.77	12.03	—11.80	2819.91	18.33
21	24.77	7.55	4.03	— 0.71	—34.63	2820.92	1.01
22	H	49.57	8.07	— 1.90	24.31	2900.97	80.05
23	34.22	—10.19	—13.35	—14.32	—34.95	2862.38	— 38.59
24	30.19	40.85	— 3.72	— 1.48	7.67	2935.89	73.51
25	—53.71	11.38	1.74	6.43	—44.55	2857.18	— 78.71
26	—12.13	— 2.72	19.80	16.58	1.98	2880.69	23.51
27	18.57	12.37	H	—32.42	25.74	2904.95	24.26
28	9.16	—23.27	41.83	37.13	10.40	2980.20	75.25
29	19.55	N/C	—18.07	12.13	—32.67	2961.14	— 19.06
30	—56.44	17.82	8.42	—10.15	—22.28	2898.51	— 62.63
31	18.82	—12.13	— 5.94	—34.66	—54.95	2809.65	— 88.86
32	—93.31	— 5.70	24.26	24.01	—42.33	2716.58	— 93.07
33	30.20	0.99	0.50	—66.83	—36.64	2644.80	— 71.78
34	11.64	—52.48	—43.81	—76.73	49.50	2532.92	—111.88
35	78.71	3.22	17.58	—39.11	21.04	2614.36	81.44
36	H	— 0.99	14.85	—31.93	23.26	2619.55	5.19
37	— 3.96	— 2.97	13.12	—43.07	—18.56	2564.11	— 55.44
38	3.22	3.96	—13.86	—39.11	— 5.94	2512.38	— 51.73
39	—59.41	32.67	—25.99	—32.17	25.00	2452.48	— 59.90
40	63.36	—10.64	—15.84	27.47	— 6.19	2510.64	58.16
41	13.12	—78.22	—37.62	—42.82	32.92	2398.02	—112.62
42	18.32	—35.15	6.68	64.85	68.07	2520.79	122.77
43	— 4.70	—22.03	10.15	—20.05	—48.02	2436.14	—84.65
44	— 5.94	17.82	— 5.69	12.62	35.89	2490.84	54.70
45	11.39	—17.08	—44.31	2.97	44.80	2488.61	— 2.23
46	51.74	— 4.95	24.25	—14.60	5.20	2550.25	61.64
47	15.10	—35.15	9.16	H	—12.13	2527.23	—23.02
48	5.94	10.64	— 8.66	—16.34	40.84	2559.65	32.42
49	5.94	14.11	30.70	— 7.92	—12.38	2590.10	30.45
50	6.68	—10.64	36.14	— 7.92	—20.55	2593.81	3.71
51	— 0.49	33.41	N/C	2.73	4.20	2633.66	39.85
52	—12.37	H	15.84	—11.63	3.71	2629.21	— 4.45
53	4.45				Year's close	2633.66	4.45*
TOTALS	**153.11**	**41.57**	**47.90**	**—330.48**	**—31.64**		**—119.54**

* Partial week

MAY

MONDAY

25

Don't compete. Create. Find out
what everyone else is doing
and then don't do it.
— Joel Weldon

15.28

TUESDAY

26

Averaging down in a bear market
is tantamount to taking a seat
on the down escalator at Macy's.
— Richard Russell,
Dow Theory Letters, 1984

15.29

WEDNESDAY

27

Big money is made in the stock market
by being on the right side of major
moves. I don't believe in
swimming against the tide.
— Martin Zweig

15.41

THURSDAY

28

The possession of gold has ruined fewer
men than the lack of it.
— Thomas Bailey Aldridge, 1903

FRIDAY

29

A man will fight harder for his interests
than his rights.
— Napoleon Bonaparte, 1815

SATURDAY

30

SUNDAY

31

O "Summer Rally" start in June
Lift my portfolio to the moon!

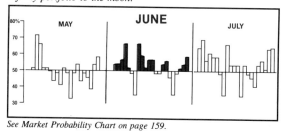

See Market Probability Chart on page 159.

JUNE ALMANAC

□ After rising just three times between 1965 and 1974, the S&P rose in eleven of the following sixteen Junes □ Autos used to begin major moves here □ RECORD: very little ground gained in 41 Junes □ 1987 was biggest June % gain since 1955, Dow was up 127 points □ Many sharp spring declines accelerate into June □ June is the leading rallying point after October during both bull and bear markets □ Best in last 10 election years up 9, down 1.

JUNE DAILY POINT CHANGES DOW JONES INDUSTRIALS

	1981	1982	1983	1984	1985	1986	1987	1988	1989	1990
Previous Month Close	991.75	819.54	1199.98	1104.85	1315.41	1876.71	2291.57	2031.12	2480.15	2876.66
1	6.21	—4.57	2.23	19.50	—	—	— 3.34	32.89	10.48	24.31
2	—10.48	1.91	9.23	—	—	—14.76	—10.01	—11.56	27.20	—
3	2.23	— 0.38	1.60	—	— 4.48	8.48	42.47	18.85	—	—
4	— 2.97	—11.52	—	7.22	4.37	— 7.14	16.39	—	—	34.22
5	7.05	—	—	— 6.68	5.26	16.15	—10.93	—	—37.13	—10.19
6	—	—	1.20	8.95	6.72	6.46	—	3.91	15.62	—13.35
7	—	— 0.95	—19.33	— 1.40	—10.86	—	—	—20.62	16.00	—14.32
8	1.85	— 1.80	— 9.41	— 1.19	—	—	25.49	48.36	4.59	—34.95
9	— 1.20	— 6.66	3.50	—	—	—45.75	1.06	— 9.60	— 3.49	—
10	— 0.56	3.14	7.11	—	2.02	— 2.96	0.91	8.36	—	—
11	13.54	11.03	—	—15.64	— 4.60	8.88	6.52	—	—	30.19
12	— 1.14	—	—	— 5.08	— 7.50	— 7.94	17.60	—	5.42	40.85
13	—	—	24.44	N/C	—16.24	36.06	—	— 2.31	—15.30	— 3.72
14	—	— 7.89	6.71	—12.92	10.86	—	—	25.07	— 0.18	— 1.48
15	5.71	— 0.58	10.02	—10.71	—	—	13.81	6.93	—28.36	7.67
16	— 8.66	— 4.37	11.02	—	— 2.42	15.81	—37.16	11.38	—	—
17	3.23	— 5.42	— 6.11	—	— 2.57	— 5.99	N/C	9.78	—	—
18	—11.41	— 2.86	—	22.75	6.38	3.16	0.78	—	—	—53.71
19	1.04	—	—	6.18	— 7.39	—13.08	12.72	—	— 6.49	11.38
20	—	—	— 3.01	15.80	2.35	23.68	—	—20.09	— 7.01	1.74
21	—	1.33	8.22	— 4.42	24.75	—	—	25.24	— 7.97	6.43
22	—	— 1.99	9.71	— 1.71	3.86	—	—	24.66	43.03	—44.55
23	12.46	13.51	— 3.90	—	—	—15.28	— 5.78	— 3.91	49.70	—
24	— 7.33	— 2.76	— 0.10	—	— 3.92	11.29	—11.32	— 5.33	—	—
25	— 2.56	— 7.33	—	— 0.55	2.47	9.50	22.64	—	—	—12.13
26	— 3.90	—	—	— 7.73	0.78	— 4.85	—14.19	—	—20.49	— 2.72
27	—	—	—12.22	— 6.07	8.40	5.06	—	—34.50	14.99	19.80
28	—	8.85	—20.24	9.83	3.25	—	—	22.41	—21.63	16.58
29	— 8.28	0.28	4.61	5.85	—	—	10.05	— 8.89	—46.47	1.98
30	— 7.71	— 0.28	8.12	—	—	7.46	—28.38	19.73	—18.21	—
Close	976.88	811.93	1221.96	1132.40	1335.46	1892.72	2418.53	2141.71	2440.06	2880.69
Change	—14.87	— 7.61	21.98	27.55	20.05	16.01	126.96	110.59	—40.09	4.03

JUNE

MONDAY

1

In all recorded history, there has not
been one economist who has had to
worry about where the next meal
would come from.
— Peter Drucker

TUESDAY

2

The less a man knows about the past
and the present the more insecure must
be his judgment of the future.
— Sigmund Freud

WEDNESDAY

3

Marx's great achievement was to place the
system of capitalism on the defensive.
— Charles A. Madison, 1977

THURSDAY

4

The word ''crisis'' in Chinese, is
composed of two characters:
the first, the symbol of danger;
the second, opportunity.

FRIDAY

5

In the course of evolution and a higher
civilization we might be able to get
along comfortably without Congress,
but without Wall Street never.
— Henry Clews, 1900

SATURDAY

6

SUNDAY

7

LAST + FIRST FOUR DAYS vs. REST OF MONTH 1983-91

If you could arrange to be invested only during the last plus the first four days of the month, you would far outperform anyone invested only during the remaining sixteen days (on average) of the month. Program trading may have affected monthly seasonality during 1985 and 1986 in the week before and after index futures expirations. Seasonality resumed when expirations were moved to early A.M.

NET DOW POINT CHANGES SHOWING MONTHLY BIAS

	Best 5 Days	Rest of Month	Best 5 Days	Rest of Month	Best 5 Days	Rest of Month
	1983		**1984**		**1985**	
Jan.	23.55	6.17	26.48	— 63.24	— 13.58	97.29
Feb.	13.16	43.03	— 47.21	— 17.17	— 7.29	0.44
Mar.	20.02	2.33	— 4.61	18.22	— 0.66	— 19.56
Apr.	—25.64	101.87	— 40.20	38.52	— 1.66	0.67
May	0.20	— 3.58	— 3.76	— 62.72	—11.93	57.99
June	— 3.10	0.80	31.25	— 5.89	21.50	4.93
July	— 3.40	5.91	— 3.98	— 7.95	2.24	11.65
Aug.	—33.26	12.95	92.98	20.32	—20.94	— 9.97
Sept.	50.10	— 6.00	— 15.90	9.38	0.56	14.90
Oct.	28.66	—45.32	— 29.37	29.92	7.95	46.83
Nov.	— 5.19	68.31	26.84	50.69	27.87	72.75
Dec.	—17.81	— 9.23	3.97	33.68	7.22	67.55
Totals	**47.29**	**165.50**	**36.49**	**— 57.62**	**11.28**	**335.01**
Average	**3.24**	**13.79**	**3.04**	**— 4.80**	**0.94**	**27.92**
	1986		**1987**		**1988**	
Jan.	15.25	— 13.63	84.44	166.96	101.79	—121.85
Feb.	48.51	113.30	41.48	15.19	— 6.47	99.64
Mar.	—17.39	125.12	59.75	1.98	34.65	— 79.74
Apr.	—82.50	86.67	127.13	—151.28	84.05	— 20.89
May	—37.94	94.40	87.93	— 31.51	—21.05	— 63.79
June	— 2.91	5.82	26.40	109.83	118.77	46.77
July	—46.26	— 59.61	2.87	117.66	0.71	— 40.36
Aug.	0.14	120.64	26.79	45.12	44.27	— 94.95
Sept.	— 0.42	—144.55	— 77.97	29.19	27.56	47.12
Oct.	29.25	93.92	— 41.94	—610.30	—11.56	40.90
Nov.	13.22	25.17	47.08	— 74.93	— 4.09	— 31.29
Dec.	22.92	— 31.07	—143.74	183.36	47.83	19.21
Totals	**—58.13**	**416.28**	**240.22**	**—198.73**	**416.46**	**—199.23**
Average	**— 4.84**	**34.69**	**20.02**	**— 16.56**	**34.71**	**— 16.61**
	1989		**1990**		**1991**	
Jan.	11.61	129.82	40.95	—230.01	—106.44	190.35
Feb.	— 3.04	— 70.71	63.07	10.81	117.82	58.17
Mar.	44.46	— 13.48	59.68	50.90	84.16	— 55.70
Apr.	10.63	127.02	— 6.53	— 76.12	6.93	— 47.52
May	—34.09	90.65	65.31	168.20		
June	20.77	— 38.05	33.09	— 32.94		
July	29.59	147.38	26.24	12.38		
Aug.	18.21	74.70	—200.99	—123.02		
Sept.	—21.27	— 11.97	26.23	—192.07		
Oct.	78.65	—170.08	89.35	— 68.81		
Nov.	—21.31	106.61	37.13	33.66		
Dec.	47.99	— 4.47	83.67	26.73		
Totals	**182.20**	**367.42**	**317.20**	**—420.29**	**102.47**	**145.30**
Average	**15.18**	**30.62**	**26.43**	**— 35.02**	**25.62**	**36.33**

		Best Five Days		Rest of Month (16 Days)	
100	Net D.J. Points	1295.48	Net D.J. Points	553.64
MONTH	Average Period	12.95	Average Period	5.54
TOTALS	Average Day	2.59	Average Day	0.35

JUNE

MONDAY
8

Pay Narberth Real Estate Taxes

Murphy @ Slota – Form 1065 – 4 Hrs ✓
Adjustments @ fill in Forms
Final adjustments still to be made

Meltdown will occur after 2 month drop
in short interest

TUESDAY
9

Murphy @ Slota   3:00 PM – 7:00 PM   4 Hrs ✓

Review of corporate adjustments
with RES & LFM

WEDNESDAY
10

Murphy, Slota @ Koropey – 1½ Hr

Murphy, @ Slota – F 1065 – Complete Forms ✓
                              4 Hrs

THURSDAY
11

Murphy @ Slota – F 1065 – Complete Forms
                          2 Hrs ✓

FRIDAY
12

SATURDAY
13

SUNDAY
14

MARKET GAINS MORE ON FIVE DAYS OF MONTH THAN ON ALL REMAINING DAYS COMBINED

Investing only on the last trading day of the month and on the first, second, third and fourth days of the following month (the "best five days") and then switching into money market funds for the remaining days of the month, alternating back and forth each month, was a smart strategy over the years until 1985.

From 1967 (Dow 786.35) to April 1991 (Dow 2924.50), the Dow Jones industrial average gained 2138.15 points. However, it is incredible that the "best five days" of the 292 months of the 24⅓ year period produced a gain of 2011.34 points in contrast to a gain of 126.81 points on the rest of the trading days (16 on average) of these months.

NET DOW POINT CHANGE FOR PRIME FIVE DAYS (1967-1991)

	JAN	FEB	MAR	APR	MAY	JUN	JUL	AUG	SEP	OCT	NOV	DEC
1967	22.39	7.01	5.56	− 8.74	7.13	− 2.27	7.11	22.24	14.45	− 2.25	−30.73	9.13
1968	3.41	1.68	− 7.51	37.40	6.19	14.92	13.84	− 6.44	26.92	22.89	− 0.43	1.92
1969	−19.39	4.54	10.51	−12.10	27.96	− 6.21	13.45	22.30	− 8.91	− 8.64	4.69	−13.99
1970	7.13	1.91	23.10	6.53	−19.00	22.38	−13.55	−11.91	5.34	21.57	18.00	34.71
1971	− 3.49	9.65	9.38	9.34	−10.76	16.37	13.58	−11.97	15.04	16.72	5.55	25.99
1972	19.42	0.30	25.89	26.42	− 8.66	−19.72	11.81	25.06	4.59	−13.85	38.38	9.33
1973	39.81	−13.02	31.08	−35.68	31.68	−10.69	−24.53	−20.99	16.10	2.63	−55.46	−20.99
1974	28.83	−37.70	16.43	4.54	9.46	41.77	−11.89	8.21	21.04	−37.39	− 3.91	−32.27
1975	37.94	17.75	30.66	−23.00	31.68	27.15	−12.04	−17.99	6.50	14.43	1.50	−29.44
1976	46.28	− 3.94	− 8.19	9.52	−12.60	− 1.67	9.49	7.39	27.67	−31.50	− 9.56	11.72
1977	−19.20	− 9.64	20.03	− 6.48	16.12	− 4.24	3.82	− 1.82	17.50	1.99	−12.74	−20.36
1978	−37.30	− 3.82	− 5.63	4.33	− 2.51	32.31	9.18	32.14	12.99	15.16	3.03	31.79
1979	25.67	−28.93	19.58	10.83	− 9.10	13.34	3.12	9.81	− 9.55	2.64	−17.33	3.33
1980	− 6.91	− 0.08	−26.37	− 9.31	4.95	12.45	16.38	2.05	10.58	43.77	14.67	−19.20
1981	16.90	− 0.51	− 9.96	− 9.63	−24.41	− 5.01	−22.73	0.57	−19.79	6.28	6.56	3.71
1982	−11.32	−17.22	−18.27	14.84	18.26	−19.98	−12.55	−16.36	20.98	37.99	59.23	52.80
1983	23.55	13.16	20.02	−25.64	0.20	− 3.10	− 3.40	−33.26	50.10	28.66	− 5.19	−17.81
1984	26.48	−47.21	− 4.61	−40.20	− 3.76	31.25	− 3.98	92.98	−15.90	−29.37	26.84	3.97
1985	−13.58	− 7.29	− 0.66	− 1.66	−11.93	21.50	2.24	−20.94	0.56	7.95	27.87	7.22
1986	15.25	48.51	−17.39	−82.50	−37.94	− 2.91	−46.26	0.14	− 0.42	29.25	13.22	22.92
1987	84.44	41.48	59.75	127.13	87.93	26.40	2.87	26.79	−77.97	−41.94	47.08	−143.74
1988	101.79	− 6.47	34.65	84.05	−21.05	118.77	0.71	44.27	27.56	−11.56	− 4.09	47.83
1989	11.61	− 3.04	44.46	10.63	−34.09	20.77	29.59	18.21	−21.27	78.65	−21.31	47.99
1990	40.95	63.07	59.68	− 6.53	65.31	33.09	26.24	−200.99	26.23	89.35	37.13	83.67
1991	−106.44	117.82	84.16	6.93								
Totals	334.22	148.01	396.35	91.02	111.06	356.67	−32.48	−30.51	150.34	243.43	143.00	100.23
Up	17	12	16	13	12	14	12	14	17	16	14	16
Down	8	13	9	12	12	10	12	10	7	8	10	8

The most Dow points during the "best five days" were gained in March (396), followed by June (356), January (334), and October (243). July was the worst month losing 32.48 Dow points.

February and July had been losers for this investment strategy in most years since 1973 (shaded).

JUNE

MONDAY
15

The worst trades are generally when
people freeze and start to pray and
hope rather than take some action.
— Robert Mnuchin,
Goldman, Sachs

TUESDAY
16

36 1/2 - 3/8
37 1/4
36 1/2

A good trader has to have three things:
a chronic inability to accept things at
face value, to feel continuously
unsettled, and to have humility.
— Michael Steinhardt

WEDNESDAY
17

36 1/8 - 3/8
32 3/4
36

The pursuit of gain is the only way
in which people can serve the needs of
others whom they do not know.
— Friedrich von Hayek,
Counterrevolution of Science

THURSDAY
18

36
36 1/2
36

Cheapening the cost of necessities
and conveniences of life is the most
powerful agent of civilization
and progress.
— Thomas Elliott Perkins, 1888

FRIDAY
19

Pulse Engineering - June BUY   36 3/8
Good BUY   36 3/4 ☠ ☠ ☠
                                 36 1/8
Meltdown will occur after
2 month drop in Short interest

In the market, yesterday is a memory and
tomorrow is a vision. And looking back
is a lot easier than looking ahead.
— Frankie Joe

SATURDAY
20

Father's Day

SUNDAY
21

SUMMER PORTFOLIO REVIEW

NO. OF SHARES	SECURITY	A ORIGINAL COST	B CURRENT VALUE	C GAIN (B-A) OR LOSS (A-B)	D % CHANGE (C÷A)	E MONTHS HELD	F CHANGE PER MO. (D÷E)	G ANNUAL RETURN (Fx12)
200	Sample Corp.	$10,000	$10,400	$400	4.0%	8	0.5%	6.0%
TOTALS								

Stocks which have achieved their potential

1

2

3

Stocks which have been disappointments

1

2

3

Candidates for addition to portfolio

1

2

3

Investment decisions

1

2

3

36 1/4
36 3/8
35 3/4

MONDAY

22

The American system of ours gives
everyone of us a great opportunity if we
only seize it with both hands.
— Al Capone, 1929

35
36 1/4
34 5/8

TUESDAY

23

Murphy & Slote
Phila Taxes
Review letter @ law
Telephone call to Morris Guerra   1 Hr

Marty Zweig's motto: Never fight
the tape, never fight the Fed.

35
35 3/8
34 3/4

WEDNESDAY

24

Major bottoms are usually made when
analysts cut their earnings estimates
and companies report earnings
which are below expectations.
— Edward Babbitt, Jr.,
Avatar Associates

BUY OEX Puts

35
35 3/4
35

THURSDAY

25

Speculation in its truest sense,
calls for anticipation.
— Richard D. Wyckoff

BUY DISNEY PUTS

Murphy & Slote

Review Accounts — loan, ins., equip., imprv, etc
Prepare journal entries
8 HRS ✓

FRIDAY

26

Italians come to ruin most generally
in three ways — women, gambling
and farming. My family chose
the slowest one.
— Pope John XXIII, 1961

SATURDAY

27

Murphy & Slote
Adjust — Leasehold Improvements and
Office Equipment Account
2 HRS ✓

SUNDAY

28

Stocks used to rocket in July, oh wow!
Came unpatriotic spoilsports, bye-bye Dow

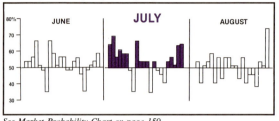

JULY
ALMANAC

JULY						
S	M	T	W	T	F	S
				1	2	3	4
5	6	7	8	9	10	11
12	13	14	15	16	17	18
19	20	21	22	23	24	25
26	27	28	29	30	31	

AUGUST						
S	M	T	W	T	F	S
						1
2	3	4	5	6	7	8
9	10	11	12	13	14	15
16	17	18	19	20	21	22
23	24	25	26	27	28	29
30	31					

See Market Probability Chart on page 159.

☐ Last 41 years July was up 14 times in first 17 years, up only 9 times in next 24 years ☐ First third far outperforms remainder of month ☐ July sixth best in S&P 500, up 1.1% on average since 1950 ☐ Best July of all time was 1989, Dow up 220.60 ☐ Great Julys during bull markets often precede October massacres 1978, 1987, 1989 or bear markets 1973, 1980 ☐ Election years so-so but tend upward if Republican candidate seems to be ahead.

JULY DAILY POINT CHANGES DOW JONES INDUSTRIALS

Previous Month	1981	1982	1983	1984	1985	1986	1987	1988	1989	1990
Close	976.88	811.93	1221.96	1132.40	1335.46	1892.72	2418.53	2141.71	2440.06	2880.69
1	− 9.22	− 8.66	3.30	—	1.68	10.82	− 8.77	−10.13	—	
2	− 8.47	− 6.28	—	− 2.32	− 3.13	5.49	26.94	—	—	18.57
3	—	—	—	4.20	− 7.62	− 8.16	—	—	12.71	12.37
4	H	H	H	H	H	H	H	H	H	H
5	—	—	−16.73	− 9.72	8.06	—	—	27.03	3.79	−32.42
6	− 9.89	1.91	12.12	− 1.99	—	—	− 7.17	−28.45	5.88	25.74
7	4.85	0.76	−10.21	—	—	−61.87	20.25	− 7.47	25.42	—
8	− 0.67	5.32	− 3.21	—	− 6.04	−18.27	14.19	−16.54	—	—
9	5.52	9.14	—	11.48	− 6.50	5.34	−12.76	—	—	9.16
10	− 3.33	—	—	− 7.17	10.98	5.76	4.78	—	14.80	−23.27
11	—	—	8.31	−18.33	4.81	−10.40	—	5.16	11.95	41.83
12	—	10.75	−17.02	− 3.98	0.90	—	—	−18.67	18.02	37.13
13	− 1.33	− 0.67	− 0.70	5.30	—	—	− 3.02	11.73	5.69	10.40
14	− 6.09	4.19	6.51	—	—	−27.98	28.38	9.25	16.50	—
15	5.90	− 1.05	−12.02	—	− 3.14	−24.75	2.39	15.83	—	—
16	1.33	1.33	—	6.96	12.43	5.48	13.23	—	—	19.55
17	3.42	—	—	6.07	10.08	7.60	13.07	—	− 1.33	N/C
18	—	—	− 2.41	−11.26	− 7.05	− 3.80	—	−11.56	− 8.73	−18.07
19	—	− 2.57	7.22	− 8.72	8.62	—	—	−20.63	39.65	12.13
20	−18.36	7.33	30.74	− 1.55	—	—	−22.32	13.34	− 8.92	−32.67
21	− 6.08	− 1.24	1.51	—	—	1.13	−19.77	−24.01	31.87	—
22	− 9.80	− 0.19	1.80	—	− 1.90	16.02	2.23	−25.60	—	—
23	3.90	− 1.43	—	− 4.75	− 5.83	3.24	1.76	—	—	−56.44
24	8.18	—	—	−10.05	− 2.91	− 6.75	13.39	—	−22.38	17.82
25	—	—	1.70	10.38	4.71	18.42	—	10.84	− 1.90	8.42
26	—	− 5.13	10.82	10.60	3.47	—	—	2.14	29.97	−10.15
27	9.13	− 2.67	−13.22	7.07	—	—	8.61	−20.27	22.38	−22.28
28	− 6.47	−10.94	−14.12	—	—	−36.14	25.83	28.63	− 0.19	—
29	− 2.00	0.38	−17.13	—	−13.22	− 7.03	19.77	46.40	—	—
30	7.71	− 3.61	—	− 4.64	2.24	12.52	27.90	—	—	18.82
31	7.23	—	—	5.30	1.35	− 4.08	4.63	—	25.42	−12.13
Close	952.34	808.60	1199.22	1115.28	1347.45	1775.31	2572.07	2128.73	2660.66	2905.20
Change	−24.54	− 3.33	−22.74	−17.12	11.99	−117.41	153.54	−12.98	220.60	24.51

MONDAY

29

PICPA - 5500 Series Conference 8:47 9:00 AM

It's no coincidence that three of the top
five stock options traders in a recent
trading contest were all ex-Marines.
— Robert Prechter, Jr.,
Elliott Wave Theorist

TUESDAY

30

Murphy @ Slota - F1120
Leasehold Improvements
Notes Payable Partnership
Fringes, etc.
Leased inclusion amount   6 HRS ✓
T & E exclusion

In nature there are no rewards or
punishments; there are consequences.
— Horace Annesley Vachell,
The Force of Clay

WEDNESDAY

1

Murphy @ Slota. - F1120
Reconcile differences
Post adjusting entries to G/L
Review ending balances

5 HRS ✓

A loss never bothers me after I take it.
I forget it overnight. But being wrong —
not taking the loss — that is what does
damage to the pocketbook and to the soul.
— Jesse Livermore

THURSDAY

2

Chadwick Funeral Home
Correction of April G/L postings
and Payroll Update for PA W/H   2 1/2 Hrs ✓
Review Life Insurance Exchange
w/ A. Keessee and Entry Possibilities   1 1/2 Hrs

The facts are unimportant! It's what they
are perceived to be that determines the
course of events.
— R. Earl Hadady

(Market Closed)

FRIDAY

3

The commodity futures game is a
money game — not a game involving
the supply-demand of the actual
commodity as commonly depicted.
— R. Earl Hadady

Independence Day

SATURDAY

4

SUNDAY

5

L.F. Murphy & R.E. Slota, Partners - F1065
Correction of Forms 1065 &
Processing of Forms 1065   2 1/2 Hrs ✓

THE ELUSIVE SUMMER RALLY

"Summer rally" is a term that has become part of Wall Street folklore. But a clearly identifiable one simply does not exist. The only honest-to-goodness rally that investors could often count on was the "midyear rally." If we set an arbitrary trading period of five days prior to July 4 and five days after, we get an average gain of 1.14 percent. This is equal to a 3-point daily gain for the nine-day period. However, since we began publishing the data annually in 1973, professionals may have been acting on this information.

THE MID-YEAR RALLY VS. REST OF JULY

Year	Five Days Prior To July 4	Five Days After July 4	Change Day Before July 4	Nine Day Net Change	Change Rest of July	Total July Change
1954	29.28*	30.12*	1.30%	2.87%	2.52%	5.7%
1955	40.99	42.75	0.39	4.29	1.80	6.1
1956	47.07	48.69	0.83	3.44	1.44	5.2
1957	47.26	48.86	1.22	3.39	−1.94	1.1
1958	44.90	45.72	0.33	1.82	3.22	4.3
1959	57.98	59.91	0.53	3.33	1.00	3.5
1960	57.33	56.87	0.25	−0.80	−2.39	−2.5
1961	64.47	65.69	0.88	1.89	1.63	3.3
1962	52.60	57.73	1.13	9.75	0.87	6.4
1963	69.07	69.76	0.69	1.00	−0.90	−0.3
1964	81.46	83.36	0.40	2.33	−0.22	1.8
1965	81.60	85.69	0.80	5.01	−0.51	1.3
1966	86.08	87.45	1.03	1.59	−4.40	−1.3
1967	91.30	92.48	0.30	1.29	2.45	4.5
1968	99.98	102.26	1.17	2.28	−4.42	−1.8
1969	97.33	95.77	0.68	−1.60	−4.11	−6.0
1970	73.47	74.57	−0.16	1.50	4.67	7.3
1971	97.74	100.82	0.00	3.15	−5.00	−3.9
1972	107.37	107.32	0.33	0.00	0.06	0.2
1973	103.62	105.80	−1.00	2.10	2.29	3.8
1974	86.31	79.89	−0.06	−7.47	−0.73	−7.8
1975	94.81	94.66	0.19	−0.16	−6.24	−6.8
1976	103.43	105.90	0.50	2.39	−2.32	−0.8
1977	100.98	99.55	−0.37	−1.42	−0.70	−1.6
1978	94.98	95.93	−0.46	1.00	4.95	5.4
1979	102.27	103.64	0.10	1.34	0.16	0.9
1980	116.00	117.84	1.54	1.59	3.25	6.5
1981	132.56	129.37	−0.87	−2.41	1.20	−0.3
1982	110.26	109.57	−0.95	−0.98	−2.26	−2.3
1983	168.46	168.11	0.48	−0.21	−3.30	−3.8
1984	151.64	150.56	0.33	−0.71	0.06	−1.6
1985	191.23	192.95	−0.29	0.90	−1.05	−0.5
1986	249.60	242.22	−0.36	−2.96	−2.52	−5.0
1987	307.16	308.37	0.89	0.39	3.33	4.8
1988	269.06	270.55	−0.63	0.55	0.54	−0.5
1989	328.44	328.78	0.44	0.10	5.26	8.8
1990	355.14	361.23	0.17	1.71	−1.57	−0.9
	Average		0.32%	1.14%	−0.10%	0.9%

*S & P composite Index

The market used to rise gloriously on the day before Independence Day but a group of unpatriotic little spoilsports (institutions) took advantage and sold into the strength in the last two decades. A good July in 1987 preceded the crash. Many other great Julys during bull markets (1973, 1978, 1980, 1987, 1989) have jinxed the market.

JULY

MONDAY
6

Murphy & Slota — F 1120   10 - 3

Life Insurance Entries —   5 HRS ✓
Update payroll program
Close out G/L & setup new year

Regulatory agencies within five years
become controlled by industries they
were set up to regulate.
— Gabriel Kolko

TUESDAY
7

Charts not only tell what was, they tell
what is; and a trend from was to is
(projected linearly into the will be)
contains better percentages
than clumsy guessing.
— R.A. Levy

WEDNESDAY
8

Murphy & Slota

Meeting — Re: Phila. Taxes
        Write Off Costs   3 HRS ✓

If a battered stock refuses to sink any
lower no matter how many negative
articles appear in the papers, that
stock is worth a close look.
— James L. Fraser,
Contrary Investor

THURSDAY
9

I know but one sure tip from a
broker…your margin call.
— Jesse Livermore

FRIDAY
10

The business world worships mediocrity.
Officially we revere free enterprise,
initiative, and individuality.
Unofficially, we fear it.
— George Lois,
Art of Advertising, 1977

SATURDAY
11

SUNDAY
12

THE WINNER OF THE 1992 ELECTION
CAN BE PREDICTED BY THE DOW'S DIRECTION

One of the best political polls can be found on Wall Street.

If the Dow Jones industrial average is higher on the Monday before Election Day than it was at the start of 1992, then a Republican president will most likely be in the White House in January 1993. If, on the other hand, the average is lower than it was New Year's Day 1992, the Democratic party will most likely take over the presidency.

Since 1900, the stock market, as represented by the thirty Dow Jones industrial stocks, has foretold a presidential victory for the party in power by gaining ground between January 1 and Election Day. Six exceptions did occur:

1) In 1912, although the market had scored a gain, Teddy Roosevelt (running on the Progressive ticket in a three-way race) split the Republican party and caused it to lose the presidency.

2) In 1940, though the market was depressed by the fall of France, the Democrats and Franklin D. Roosevelt were still able to win the election and a third term.

3) In 1968 this indicator failed, but it never really had a chance to show its stuff due to a third party in the race and President Johnson's withdrawal as a candidate.

4) Despite no recession and a rising Dow in 1976, the Republicans narrowly lost, thanks to the twin nightmares of Watergate and the OPEC-induced worldwide recession in 1974.

5) The party in power was ousted in 1980 though the market rose. Carter was doomed by the Ayatollah.

6) Despite lower prices in the first seven months of 1984, the Dow recovered by Election Day and just missed (by ten points) getting back to where it was on January 1.

Though this indicator was vindicated in 1988 when a rising market between New Year's Day and Election Day presaged a Republican victory, it is difficult to ignore its three bad calls in a row in 1976, 1980 and 1984.

Extraordinary exogenous events such as Watergate and the resignation of a president in 1974 and the psychologically devastating seizure of the US embassy in Iran and its personnel in 1979 completely overpowered this indicator in the 1976 and 1980 elections.

Important in 1984 was the market's preceding rise from August 12, 1982 at Dow 776.92 to 1287.20 on November 29, 1983, a very substantial gain of 65.7%. The election-predicting indicator became irrelevent when the market declined only 13.7% by its July 24, 1984 mini-bear market low. Such a puny decline after a huge rise was not about to hamper Reagan's landslide re-election.

To put this all in perspective for 1991, let's assume the Dow has a similar 65.7% move from the October 11, 1990 low of 2365.10. This takes us up to 3918 by year-end 1991. Then the Dow drops 13.7% as in 1984 to 3382.07. This scenario would not likely affect a Bush re-election.

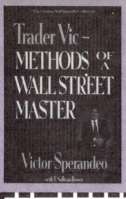

BEST INVESTMENT BOOK 1992

As a special service to Almanac readers, we offer you the opportunity to purchase TRADER VIC—METHODS OF A WALL STREET MASTER by Victor Sperandeo, the 1992 Best Investment Book of the Year (see review pages 82-85). Victor Sperandeo covers everything you need for success in the financial markets: the right knowledge, a method of implementation, and the proper psychology.

RESERVE YOUR 1993 STOCK TRADER'S ALMANAC NOW!

☐ Please reserve _____ copies of next year's Twenty-Sixth Edition, The 1993 STOCK TRADER'S ALMANAC. $26.00 plus $4.00 postage and handling enclosed. (Foreign & Canada, add $12.00, quantity prices available on request.)

☐ $_____ payment enclosed

Charge Credit Card (check one)

☐ VISA ☐ MasterCard ☐ AmEx

Name

Address

Account #

City

Expiration Date

State _____ Zip _____

Signature

☐ Please rush a copy of TRADER VIC—METHODS OF A WALL STREET MASTER, this year's Best Investment Book—only $28.95 (includes postage and handling). Foreign & Canada, add $15.00.

☐ Send _____ additional copies of the 1992 STOCK TRADER'S ALMANAC only $26.00 plus $4.00 shipping each. Foreign & Canada, add $12.00.

☐ $_____ payment enclosed

Charge Credit Card (check one)

☐ VISA ☐ MasterCard ☐ AmEx

Name

Address

Account #

City

Expiration Date

State _____ Zip _____

Signature

✱ ✱ TWENTY-SIXTH ✱ ✱ ANNUAL ✱ ✱ EDITION ✱ ✱

of the 1993 Stock Trader's Almanac will be published in late September 1992. Mail the postpaid card below to reserve your copy of this Edition.

JULY

MONDAY
13

10:20
11:00 Kromev 1½ Hrs
Review
estate matters

TUESDAY
14

Jones Profit Sharing Plan   6 Hrs,
Convert & Assemble SPA & Memo
Summary of Plan Activity Worksheet

WEDNESDAY
15

Jones Profit Sharing Plan   3 Hrs
Summary of Plan Activity — Completion
SPD Completion & Mail

THURSDAY
16

FRIDAY
☠ 17

SATURDAY
18

SUNDAY
19

INCUMBENT VICTORIES VS. INCUMBENT DEFEATS

As we discussed on page 64, the Dow Jones industrial average (with just six exceptions) has foretold the outcome of presidential elections in this century. When the venerable average gains ground between New Year's Day and Election Day, the incumbent party will usually win the election. A loss in the average during the period will usually result in the "ins" being ousted.

The chart below (designed by the late Ralph A. Rotnem of Smith Barney, Harris Upham) tells the story. The Dow tends to move up and gain 15.1% on average, based on the fifteen elections when the incumbent party retained the presidency. An average loss of 1.5% ensued when the incumbents lost (eight times).

The lower line is somewhat distorted by the roller-coaster market in 1932 (see monthly % changes in election years on page 96): April, down 20.2%; May, down 23.3%; July, up 37.7%; August, up 37.5%. The upper line is also distorted by the inclusion of May 1940—France fell to Germany, driving the S&P down 24.0% and the Dow down 21.7%.

STOCK PRICE TREND IN ELECTION YEARS, 1900-1988

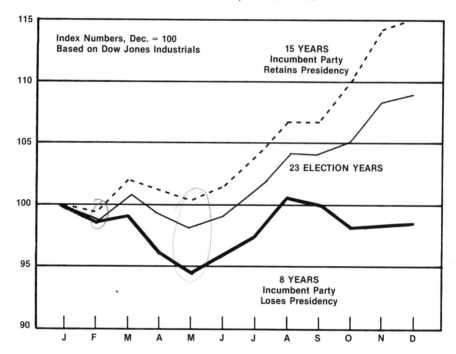

There have been four notable strong market months: March, up eighteen times, down five times; June and August, up sixteen times, down seven times; and often November, especially when Republicans are victorious.

Looking at the center graph line of the average of all 23 presidential election years, one can see which half of the average election year tends to be stronger.

JULY

MONDAY 20

City of Philadelphia — Murphy & Slote
Other — Continue zeros, etc ✓
Pickup & telephone
Chadwick Funeral Home   PST —
                          2 HRS
Work Sheet

P/B — Journal   2 HRS

TUESDAY 21

Jones Termite & Pest Control
Review Plan Documents / Forfeture Provisions
Prepare Form 5500 C/K
Change in Contribution
Telephone Calls   3 HRS

WEDNESDAY 22

THURSDAY 23

FRIDAY 24

SATURDAY 25

SUNDAY 26

HOW THE GOVERNMENT MANIPULATES
THE ECONOMY TO STAY IN POWER

Most sophisticated investors know that bull markets tend to occur in the third and fourth years of presidential terms while markets tend to decline in the first and second years.

The "making of presidents" is invariably accompanied by an unsubtle manipulation of the economy. Incumbent administrations are duty-bound to retain the reins of power. Subsequently, the "piper must be paid," producing what I have coined the "Post-Presidential Year Syndrome." Most big, bad bear markets began in such years—1929, 1937, 1957, 1969, 1973, 1977 and 1981. Note, also, that our major wars began in years following elections—Civil War (1865), WWI (1917), WWII (1941) and Vietnam (1965).

Some cold hard facts to prove economic manipulation appeared in a book by Edward R. Tufte, **Political Control of the Economy**, Princeton University Press, Princeton, N.J. The author investigated the timing of stimulative fiscal measures designed to increase per capital disposable income—which would have provided a sense of well-being to the voting public. Measures included: increases in federal budget deficits, government spending and social security benefits; interest rate reductions on government loans; and speed-ups of projected funding. Some of the findings were:

Federal Spending During 1962-1973, the average increase was 29% higher in election years than in non-election years.

Social Security There were nine increases during the 1952-1974 period. Half of the six election-year increases became effective in September, perfectly timed to remain fresh in voters' minds as they went to the polls eight weeks later. Three increases in non-election years took effect in January. The average increase was 100% higher in presidential than in midterm election years.

Real Disposable Income Accelerated in all but one election year between 1947 and 1973 (excluding the Eisenhower years). Only one of the remaining odd-numbered years (1973) showed a marked acceleration.

These moves were obviously not coincidences and explain why we tend to have a political (four-year) stock market cycle. To paraphrase Gilbert and Sullivan, we're not the very model of a modern free economy.

The Reagan administration was no different than the others. We paid the piper in 1981 and 1982 and then came the longest peacetime expansion in history—eight straight years. We temporarily repealed the four-year cycle and avoided any recessions. However, we ran up more deficits than the total deficits of the previous 200 years of our national existence.

Partisan Alan Greenspan took over the Fed from Paul Volker in 1989 and was able to keep the economy rolling until an exogenous event in the Persian Gulf pushed us into a real recession in August 1990.

Past history tells us that the incumbent will somehow manage to prevent the economy from collapsing and win reelection in 1992. Only thrice in this century have incumbents failed to retain power: Taft in 1912 when the Republican Party split in two; Hoover in 1932 when we were in the depths of the Great Depression; and Carter in 1980 during the Iran/Hostage Crisis.

Will the Post-Presidential Year Syndrome strike in 1993?

JULY/AUGUST

MONDAY
27

It's not what you say.
It's what they hear.
— A sign in an advertising office.

TUESDAY
28

I've never been poor, only broke. Being
poor is a frame of mind. Being broke is
only a temporary situation.
— Mike Todd, 1958

WEDNESDAY
29

I believe in the exceptional man — the
entrepreneur who is always out of money,
not the bureaucrat who generates cash
flow and pays dividends.
— Armand Erpf

THURSDAY
30

History is a collection of
agreed upon lies.
— Voltaire

FRIDAY
31

When I have to depend upon hope
in a trade, I get out of it.
— Jesse Livermore

SATURDAY
1

SUNDAY
2

August 25th peaked ere the '87 Crash
Smart the investor who snuck into cash

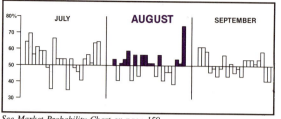

AUGUST ALMANAC

AUGUST						
S	M	T	W	T	F	S
						1
2	3	4	5	6	7	8
9	10	11	12	13	14	15
16	17	18	19	20	21	22
23	24	25	26	27	28	29
30	31					

SEPTEMBER						
S	M	T	W	T	F	S
		1	2	3	4	5
6	7	8	9	10	11	12
13	14	15	16	17	18	19
20	21	22	23	24	25	26
27	28	29	30			

See Market Probability Chart on page 159.

☐ Ignore articles extolling August bullishness since 1900—August was up 80% of the time in the first half century but only half of the time thereafter ☐ Chance for weakness greatest in latter part of month ☐ Last 3 days before Labor Day up 23 times in 30 years (pg. 76) ☐ As many declines as rallies have begun here ☐ RECORD: S&P 22 up, 19 down. Average gain 0.3% ☐ When conventions end, uncertainty ends, and stocks tend to rise in election years.

AUGUST DAILY POINT CHANGES DOW JONES INDUSTRIALS

	1981	1982	1983	1984	1985	1986	1987	1988	1989	1990
Previous Month Close	952.34	808.60	1199.22	1115.28	1347.45	1775.31	2572.07	2128.73	2660.66	2905.20
1	—	—	− 5.01	19.33	8.17	−11.67	—	1.78	−19.54	− 5.94
2	—	13.51	− 6.21	31.47	− 2.57	—	—	0.71	16.32	−34.66
3	− 6.09	− 5.71	9.82	36.00	—	—	−14.99	2.85	4.17	−54.95
4	− 0.28	−12.94	−14.73	—	—	6.33	−10.36	− 7.47	− 8.16	—
5	7.61	− 7.61	0.20	—	− 6.16	7.03	19.93	− 7.47	—	—
6	− 0.67	−11.51	—	0.88	−21.73	2.53	27.58	—	—	−93.31
7	−10.37	—	—	1.66	− 0.12	6.75	− 2.23	—	41.54	− 5.70
8	—	—	−20.23	− 8.51	4.82	− 3.66	—	−11.73	4.18	24.26
9	—	− 3.99	5.21	27.94	− 9.07	—	—	−28.27	−13.09	24.01
10	1.14	− 1.05	7.71	− 5.96	—	—	43.84	−44.99	26.55	−42.33
11	5.62	− 2.09	− 1.59	—	—	28.54	44.64	5.16	−28.64	—
12	− 4.09	− 0.29	8.44	—	− 6.50	24.33	−11.16	− 1.78	—	—
13	− 0.86	11.13	—	1.99	1.01	9.00	22.17	—	—	30.20
14	− 7.42	—	—	− 5.97	1.68	0.42	− 6.06	—	6.07	0.99
15	—	—	10.67	−15.13	0.78	10.69	—	−33.25	9.86	0.50
16	—	4.38	− 3.05	10.16	− 5.04	—	—	17.24	5.51	−66.83
17	−10.18	38.81	16.05	2.76	—	—	15.14	4.45	−13.66	−36.64
18	− 2.38	− 1.81	−14.02	—	—	13.92	−45.91	1.07	8.34	—
19	2.09	9.14	1.73	—	− 0.22	− 6.61	11.16	−11.03	—	—
20	1.91	30.72	—	5.08	11.20	18.42	40.97	—	—	11.64
21	− 7.80	—	—	22.75	5.83	− 0.14	2.71	—	−40.97	−52.48
22	—	—	8.94	− 7.95	−11.43	6.61	—	−25.78	3.99	−43.81
23	—	21.88	−10.26	0.66	0.22	—	—	− 0.89	27.12	−76.73
24	−20.46	−16.27	− 8.64	4.09	—	—	−12.43	37.34	56.53	49.50
25	1.72	9.99	0.81	—	—	−16.03	25.35	−15.82	− 2.28	—
26	− 2.57	7.52	7.01	—	0.67	32.48	−20.57	6.58	—	—
27	−10.18	− 8.94	—	8.61	4.82	0.28	−26.79	—	—	78.71
28	3.14	—	—	4.19	8.62	− 4.36	−35.71	—	11.00	3.22
29	—	—	2.04	− 5.19	4.04	− 1.83	—	24.00	−16.73	17.58
30	—	9.83	1.93	− 3.64	− 1.12	—	—	− 3.20	1.52	−39.11
31	−10.75	8.01	20.12	1.10	—	—	23.60	− 6.58	9.12	21.04
Close	881.47	901.31	1216.16	1224.38	1334.01	1898.34	2662.95	2031.65	2737.27	2614.36
Change	−70.87	92.71	16.94	109.10	−13.44	123.03	90.88	−97.08	76.61	−290.84

AUGUST

MONDAY
3

Statements by high officials are practically
always misleading when they are
designed to bolster a falling market.
— Gerald M. Loeb

TUESDAY
4

Companies which do well generally
tend to report (their quarterly earnings)
earlier than those which do poorly.
— Alan Abelson, *Barron's*

WEDNESDAY
5

No profession requires more hard
work, intelligence, patience, and mental
discipline than successful speculation.
— Robert Rhea

THURSDAY
6

Live beyond your means; then you're
forced to work hard, you have to succeed.
— Edward G. Robinson

FRIDAY
7

I have a simple philosophy.
Fill what's empty. Empty what's full.
And scratch where it itches.
— Alice Roosevelt Longworth

SATURDAY
8

SUNDAY
9

HOW TO BECOME A SUCCESSFUL INVESTOR/TRADER

One of the most valuable sections in "Trader Vic—Methods of a Wall Street Master" (page 82) focuses on the tools an individual needs to consistently win in the market. Victor Sperandeo is uniquely qualified to comment on this area. Once again, he has done his homework— reading over 200 books on psychology, personal discipline and excellence. Some excerpts of his ideas:

We have a choice: We can decide to take control over our lives and succeed, or we can give in to fear and pain and let other people and events control us. The right choice is obvious, and making it begins with one simple commitment: CARPE DIEM! (Latin, "Seize the Day!"). This means commit yourself to the fact that each moment in life is precious, is yours, and is to be experienced with as much awareness and passion as you are capable of. It means recognize that, at any moment and in any situation, you can begin the process of change required to be and feel successful. It means grasp on to life and take hold with a devoted grip that clings to unlimited possibility. Seize the day. Dream, but dream with the conviction that you can harness the power within you and turn your dreams into reality.

To trade well you have to: 1) establish goals; 2) acquire knowledge of the markets; 3) define rules of trading that work; and 4) execute in strict adherence to the rules.

The prerequisites for success consist of these personal attributes:

Self-confidence—a realization that your mind can learn the truth and apply it with positive results in every realm of life.

Self-motivation and commitment—the ability and willingness to put the time and energy into learning what to trade and how to trade it.

Intellectual independence—the ability to stand on your own judgment in the face of countervailing opinion.

Personal honesty—a total commitment to identifying and dealing with the truth about yourself, the markets, and your decisions.

A sincere love of what you do—the recognition that the greatest reward comes from the process of the work itself, not the money or fame that may come with it.

With the right motivation and commitment every human being living in a free country has the opportunity to achieve both personal fulfillment and financial attainment.

AUGUST

MONDAY
10

[S - Davenport] Vanguard

Lack of money is the root of all evil.
— George Bernard Shaw

TUESDAY
11

Murphy & Slote

Form 1120 - Account Analysis

2 Hours ✓

A statistician is someone who can draw
a straight line from an unwarranted
assumption to a foregone conclusion.

WEDNESDAY
12

Murphy & Slota

Form 1120 - Account Analysis

2 Hours ✓

In investing, the return you want
should depend on whether you
want to eat well or sleep well.
— J. Kenfield Morley

THURSDAY
13

Murphy & Slota

Form 1120 Preparation

4 Hours ✓

Those who are of the opinion that money
will do everything may very well be
suspected to do everything for money.
— Sir George Savile

FRIDAY
14

Murphy & Slote

Form PA Ret Prep

2 Hours

Photo copying   2 Hours

Engagement Letter   1 Hour   ✓

All you need is look over the earnings
forecasts publicly made a year ago to
see how much care you need to give
those being made now for next year.
— Gerald M. Loeb

SATURDAY
15

SUNDAY
16

MARKET ACTS AS A BAROMETER BETWEEN THE LAST CONVENTION AND ELECTION DAY

Another election-year phenomenon, one with an outstanding track record is the Post-Convetion-to-Election-Day Forecaster. Here the direction of the Dow between the close of the last presidential convention and Election Day reflects voter sentiment.

Of the fifteen presidential elections since 1900 where the incumbent parties were victorious, thirteen were foretold by rising stock prices. The two exceptions were minor (—0.5% in 1948 and —2.3% in 1956). Gains for the period averaged 7.8%. Conversely, dissatisfaction with an incumbent party is most times reflected by a decline between the last convention and Election Day. Here, five out of eight election years produced declines.

Though the average change when incumbent parties lost is +4.8%, it reflects the Dow hitting bottom in 1932—an 89.2% loss since 1929—then moving up over 100% intraday in 60 days before giving back half by Election Day. Excluding 1932 changes the average to minus 1.5%.

Even 1968's postconvention gain is suspect because riots and two assassinations disrupted the market and depressed it prior to the last convention.

POST-CONVENTION-TO-ELECTION MARKETS

Year Incumbent Party Won	% Change	Year Incumbent Party Lost	% Change
1900	8.3%	1912	—1.8%
1904	22.6	1920	—9.1
1908	9.6	1932	48.6
1916	15.9	1952	—2.8
1924	6.7	1960	—3.1
1928	22.4	1968	5.6
1936	11.5	1976	—0.8
1940	9.9	1980	1.4
1944	0.8	**Average**	**4.8%**
1948	—0.5	Excluding 1932	—1.5%
1956	—2.3		
1964	4.8		
1972	1.5	% change based on Dow Jones industrial average.	
1984	1.0		
1988	5.4		
Average	**7.8%**		

I PREDICT THE CANDIDATES WILL BE

Democrat _____   Republican _____

The winner of the Presidency will be _____

	Dow Close After Last Convention	Dow Close on Day Before Election	

AUGUST

MONDAY
17

It matters little what you believe, so long
as you don't altogether believe it.
— Bertrand Russell

TUESDAY
18

When a company reports higher earnings
for its first quarter (over its previous
year's first quarter), chances are almost
five to one it will also have increased
earnings in its second quarter.
— Niederhoffer, Cross & Zeckhauser

WEDNESDAY
19

I'm a great believer in luck, and I find the
harder I work the more I have of it.
— Thomas Jefferson

THURSDAY
20

The price of a stock varies inversely with
the thickness of its research file.
— Martin Sosnoff

FRIDAY
21

Money makes money. And the money that
money makes makes more money.
— Benjamin Franklin

SATURDAY
22

SUNDAY
23

LAST THREE DAYS BEFORE LABOR DAY UP 23 TIMES IN 30 YEARS

Summer is drawing to a close. Vacationers are returning home or taking one last fling. Spirits have been rejuvenated. A new business season and school year are about to begin. The air is filled with a sense of anticipation, optimism, and even euphoria. A happy setting indeed, and very likely the simple reason for eighteen straight years of rising markets during the three-day period prior to Labor Day, until 1978. My publicizing this phenomenon may have jinxed it.

Chances of an up market on these Mondays or Tuesdays have been about two in five (26 out of 60). In contrast, on Wednesday, Thursday or Friday, the odds were two to one the market would rise on any of the three days (60 out of 89).

As you can see, these three ''bullish'' days wound up in the minus column in seven of the past thirteen years. This is disappointing after an eighteen-year winning streak. However, to spotlight a brief three-day bullish bias is to doom it to subsequent failure. How could traders on stock and index future exchange floors have resisted more than a 1 percent gain on average for just three trading days? That's a return of 7 percent a month and over 100 percent a year compounded. Besides, they don't pay commissions and can trade on very low margins.

WEEK BEFORE LABOR DAY DAILY DOW POINT CHANGES

YEAR	MON	TUES	WED	THURS	FRI	WEEK'S CLOSE	CHANGE LAST 3 DAYS
1961	— 0.69	— 1.86	2.75	3.04	1.25	721.19	7.04
1962	— 1.17	— 7.32	— 2.01	— 0.92	6.86	609.18	3.93
1963	1.03	— 4.29	5.19	1.33	2.92	729.32	9.44
1964	— 0.61	5.52	1.08	0.94	2.29	848.31	4.31
1965	— 0.33	— 2.53	0.50	6.80	7.57	907.97	14.87
1966	—13.53	8.69	12.69	3.68	— 4.40	787.69	11.97
1967	0.64	0.05	— 1.04	7.57	— 0.11	901.18	6.42
1968	3.79	— 2.48	Closed	0.68	1.68	896.01	2.36
1969	— 5.81	— 7.92	1.26	3.63	8.31	836.72	13.20
1970	— 1.23	— 6.43	— 1.51	8.63	5.88	771.15	13.00
1971	— 6.72	— 3.36	0.95	1.61	12.12	912.75	14.68
1972	— 2.41	— 2.25	3.16	5.87	6.32	970.05	15.35
1973	7.22	1.36	11.36	— 0.90	5.04	887.57	15.50
1974	— 1.33	—16.59	— 4.93	— 9.77	21.74	678.58	7.04
1975	7.58	— 9.23	3.91	22.45	5.87	835.34	32.23
1976	4.99	4.82	12.21	— 1.16	4.32	989.11	15.37
1977	8.67	— 5.20	2.60	3.37	7.45	872.31	13.42
1978	—10.65	— 4.68	0.52	— 3.90	2.51	879.33	— 0.87
1979	5.21	— 0.77	0.26	— 1.20	3.93	887.63	2.99
1980	— 1.96	— 2.82	—10.32	—12.71	2.21	932.59	—20.82
1981	—10.75	1.24	1.52	—17.22	— 5.33	861.68	—21.03
1982	9.83	8.01	— 6.26	14.35	15.73	940.49	23.82
1983	2.04	1.93	20.12	— 9.35	8.64	1215.45	19.41
1984	— 8.61	4.19	— 5.19	— 3.64	1.10	1224.38	— 7.73
1985	— 0.67	4.82	8.62	4.04	— 1.12	1334.01	11.54
1986	—16.03	32.48	0.28	— 4.36	— 1.83	1898.34	— 5.91
1987	23.60	—51.98	— 8.93	— 2.55	—38.11	2561.38	—49.59
1988	24.00	— 3.20	— 6.58	—29.34	52.28	2054.59	16.36
1989	11.00	—16.73	1.52	9.12	14.82	2752.09	25.46
1990	78.71	3.22	17.58	—39.11	21.04	2614.36	— 0.49
UP	14	12	20	16	24		23
DOWN	16	18	9	14	6		7

AUGUST

MONDAY
24

The fewer analysts who follow a situation,
the more pregnant its possibilities...if
Wall Street hates a stock, buy it.
— Martin T. Sosnoff

TUESDAY
25

A bank is a place where they lend you an
umbrella in fair weather and ask for it
back again when it begins to rain.
— Robert Frost

WEDNESDAY
26

In a bull market, an "overbought"
condition typically lasts longer, while an
"oversold" condition ends very quickly.
The reverse is true in bear markets.
— Alan R. Shaw

THURSDAY
27

Buy H&R Block Puts

My son, my son, if you knew with
what little wisdom the world is ruled.
— Oxenstierna (Thirty Years' War)

FRIDAY
28

If buying equities seem the most
hazardous and foolish thing you could
possibly do, then you are near the
bottom that will end the bear market.
— Joseph E. Granville

SATURDAY
29

SUNDAY
30

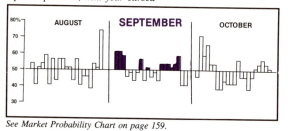

September Barometer works in reverse
Up in September, next year cursed

See Market Probability Chart on page 159.

SEPTEMBER ALMANAC

	SEPTEMBER					
S	M	T	W	T	F	S
		1	2	3	4	5
6	7	8	9	10	11	12
13	14	15	16	17	18	19
20	21	22	23	24	25	26
27	28	29	30			

	OCTOBER					
S	M	T	W	T	F	S
				1	2	3
4	5	6	7	8	9	10
11	12	13	14	15	16	17
18	19	20	21	22	23	24
25	26	27	28	29	30	31

☐ First half tends to be stronger than second half ☐ September is a "reverse" barometer of the following year (pg. 90) ☐ RECORD: S&P up 17, down 24 ☐ Average September loses 0.7% ☐ Dow up only 4 times in last 22 years, 1973, 1976, 1983 and 1988 ☐ September tends to be a bear month in election years but bullish if Republicans are ahead.

SEPTEMBER DAILY POINT CHANGES DOW JONES INDUSTRIALS

Previous Month Close	1981	1982	1983	1984	1985	1986	1987	1988	1989	1990
	881.47	901.31	1216.16	1224.38	1334.01	1898.34	2662.95	2031.65	2737.27	2614.36
1	1.24	— 6.26	— 9.35	—	—	H	—51.98	—29.34	14.82	—
2	1.52	14.35	8.64	—	H	—27.98	— 8.93	52.28	—	—
3	—17.22	15.73	—	H	— 4.82	10.97	— 2.55	—	—	H
4	— 5.33	—	—	—12.03	— 2.47	38.38	—38.11	—	H	— 0.99
5	—	—	H	— 3.32	— 0.89	—19.96	—	H	— 7.41	14.85
6	—	H	23.27	9.83	9.86	—	—	10.67	—24.89	—31.93
7	H	—10.85	5.39	—11.48	—	—	H	0.53	—12.91	23.26
8	—10.56	1.47	2.03	—	—	—11.11	—16.26	— 2.67	2.66	—
9	2.76	— 3.22	— 6.40	—	3.58	— 4.50	4.15	5.69	—	—
10	8.56	— 5.71	—	— 4.86	— 5.82	— 4.64	26.78	—	—	— 3.96
11	10.37	—	—	— 4.53	—14.01	—86.61	32.69	—	— 5.13	— 2.97
12	—	—	—10.67	2.32	— 7.05	—34.17	—	3.56	2.85	13.12
13	—	11.87	— 4.98	27.94	— 4.71	—	—	10.67	—27.74	—43.07
14	— 6.66	4.32	5.38	9.27	—	—	4.30	17.60	—14.63	—18.56
15	— 7.80	7.45	—14.43	—	—	8.86	—46.46	— 8.36	9.69	—
16	— 6.75	— 2.66	10.67	—	1.46	10.96	—36.39	5.87	—	—
17	—11.51	—10.86	—	— 0.44	—10.98	— 9.14	— 2.29	—	—	3.22
18	— 3.90	—	—	—10.82	2.24	4.78	— 3.26	—	12.92	3.96
19	—	—	8.23	—13.25	6.39	—11.53	—	—17.07	— 0.19	—13.86
20	—	— 0.64	15.25	3.53	— 8.85	—	—	6.40	— 3.42	—39.11
21	10.37	18.49	— 5.90	—14.80	—	—	—31.82	3.02	— 3.61	— 5.94
22	— 0.86	— 7.18	14.23	—	—	30.80	75.23	—10.49	1.33	—
23	— 4.76	— 1.84	— 1.93	—	18.37	4.36	17.62	10.67	—	—
24	— 5.80	— 6.25	—	3.32	4.81	5.48	—19.25	—	—	—59.41
25	—11.13	—	—	2.10	— 9.07	—34.73	3.75	—	—22.42	32.67
26	—	—	5.18	4.96	8.74	1.13	—	— 5.51	4.75	—25.99
27	—	1.38	—12.80	4.64	H*	—	—	— 2.84	9.12	—32.17
28	18.55	— 1.57	— 6.00	—10.05	—	—	31.33	3.20	21.85	25.00
29	5.33	—13.06	— 1.83	—	—	—14.49	—10.93	33.78	— 2.09	—
30	2.09	—10.02	— 7.01	—	7.84	12.38	5.71	— 6.40	—	—
Close	849.98	896.25	1233.13	1206.71	1328.63	1767.58	2596.28	2112.91	2692.82	2452.48
Change	—31.49	— 5.06	16.97	—17.67	— 5.38	—130.76	—66.67	81.26	—44.45	—161.88

*Hurricane Gloria

MONDAY
31

If a man can see both sides of a
problem, you know that none
of his money is tied up in it.
— Verda Ross

TUESDAY
1

Knowledge born from actual experience
is the answer to why one profits; lack
of it is the reason one loses.
— Gerald M. Loeb

WEDNESDAY
2

Those companies that the market
expects will have the best futures, as
measured by the price/earnings ratios
they are accorded, have consistently
done worst subsequently.
— David Dreman

THURSDAY
3

People's spending habits depend more on
how wealthy they feel than with the actual
amount of their current income.
— A.C. Pigou

FRIDAY
4

Small volume is usually accompanied
by a fall in price; large volume
by a rise in price.
— Charles C. Ying (Computer Study)

SATURDAY
5

SUNDAY
6

GOLDS GREAT BUYS SINCE 1963
DURING FOURTH QUARTERS

Fourth quarters in most of the years since 1963 have produced attractive buying opportunities for gold stocks. I noted in 1975 that catching these seasonal lows in ASA and selling at the spring or summer highs would have produced an average annual gain of 87.8% for the prior decade. The annual International Monetary Fund meetings in the fall and fourth quarter weakness in gold shares appeared to have some correlation. Arrows on the ASA chart illustrate most of the annual seasonal buy points. Ian McAvity of *Deliberations* identified a six-year gold cycle with tops in 1967-68 (after tripling), 1973-74 (after quintupling) and 1979-80 (after quadrupling). The three cycles were accompanied by the inflationary Vietnam escalation and OPEC's crippling oil price increases in 1973 and 1979. Obviously, the six-year cycle is no more. But note that giant moves began in 1978, 1982 and 1986, four years apart and all mid-term election years. I also pointed out that 1990 could make a gold statistician's dream come true.

Paul Tudor Jones in *Barron's* (July 1, 1991) believes "*The* trade for the second half of the year, possibly *the* trade for the next couple of years, is to buy gold and sell stocks." Rationale? Back in 1980, gold rose to over $800 an ounce when the Dow was at the 800 level. Since then, the ratio of gold's price to the Dow has fallen to 13%.

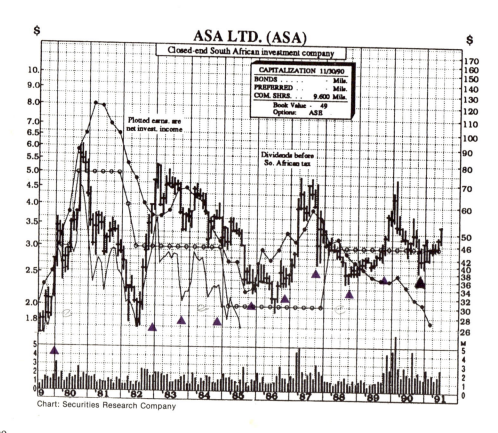

ASA LTD. (ASA)

Closed-end South African investment company

CAPITALIZATION 11/30/90
BONDS . . . . · Mils.
PREFERRED . . · Mils.
COM. SHRS. . . 9.600 Mils.
Book Value · 49
Options: ASE

Plotted earns. are net invest. income

Dividends before So. African tax

Chart: Securities Research Company

SEPTEMBER

MONDAY
7

Labor Day
(Market Closed)

I do not rule Russia;
ten thousand clerks do.
— Nicholas I (1795-1855)

TUESDAY
8

Under capitalism man exploits man:
under socialism the reverse is true.
— Polish Proverb

WEDNESDAY
9

A gold mine is a hole in the
ground with a liar on top.
— Mark Twain

THURSDAY
10

Baron Rothchild's success formula:
"I never buy at the bottom and
I always sell too soon."

FRIDAY
11

Multiple Projects Objectives c Deadlines

I prefer to be a gold bug rather
than a paper worm.
— Nicholas Deak

SATURDAY
12

SUNDAY
13

TRADER VIC—METHODS OF A WALL STREET MASTER BY VICTOR SPERANDEO BEST INVESTMENT BOOK OF THE YEAR

You'll never again have a losing year in the market if you study this new work by Victor Sperandeo. In the future when market writers recommend a few important investment books, one likely to be on most lists is "Trader Vic—Methods of a Wall Street Master." Rarely do market masters divulge their market discoveries and trading methods. Sperandeo does, just in time for our 25th Anniversary Edition "Best Investment Book of the Year" award.

Background

Victor Sperandeo's 25 years as a master stock trader were preceded by five years as a teenage poker whiz—he had been inspired by John Scarne's book on cards. Sperandeo was befriended by memorization expert Harry Lorayne, who taught him the secrets of memorization.

In 1965 at age 20, Victor worked as a quote boy at Pershing & Co. After enrolling in night school at Queens College for economics and finance, he moved to the statistics desk at Standard & Poor's. The following year Victor landed a position at Lehman Brothers where he maintained records for 12 of 32 partners. This is where he learned all about stock options by watching what the Lehman partners were doing.

Between 1968 and 1970 Sperandeo horse-traded options at Filer Schmidt and then at U.S. Options. When he suggested hedging on the short side, using puts instead of shorting stocks, a client gave Sperandeo $50,000 to try his system. Leery of putting him on salary during a bear market, U.S. Options offered Sperandeo a percentage of the spread on each contract he filled. But when he was halfway to making $100,000 for the year, the firm reneged and put him on salary. He quit to manage a stock/options portfolio on a 50% profit basis at Marsh Block. In 1971 Sperandeo started Ragnar Options Corp. and stayed till 1976, 15 months after Weeden & Co. took it over.

Dow Theory

Disappointed at missing the October 1974 bottom, Sperandeo spent all his spare time during the next two years studying Dow Theory. He classified every short-, intermediate-, and long-term move since 1896 for the Dow Jones industrial and rail (now transportation) averages. Sperandeo worked out actuarial tables logging the extent of moves (how big) and their duration (how long). This was a monumental task but it shows how much homework a dedicated trader/speculator will do to put the odds in his favor.

Sperandeo found that Dow Theory tactics accurately captured an average of 74.5% of business expansion price movements and 62% of recession price declines from confirmation date to market peaks or bottoms, respectively. He also discovered the stock market accurately predicted changes in the business trend with a median lead time of six months and anticipated peaks and troughs of business cycles with a median lead time of one month. A strict interpretation of Dow Theory from 1949 to 1985 resulted in a 20.1% uncompounded average annual return.

(continued on page 84)

SEPTEMBER

MONDAY
14

Next to being shot at and missed,
nothing is really quite as satisfying
as an income tax refund.
— F.J. Raymond

TUESDAY
15

Selling a soybean contract short is
worth two years at the
Harvard Business School.
— Robert Stovall

WEDNESDAY
16

History shows that once the United States
government fully recognizes an economic
problem and thereby places all its
efforts on solving it, the problem is
about to be solved by natural forces.
— James L. Fraser

THURSDAY
17

A committee is a group of the
unprepared, appointed by the
unwilling, to do the unnecessary.
— Fred Allen

FRIDAY
18

Foreign Aid: taxing poor people
in rich countries for the benefit of
rich people in poor countries.
— Bernard Rosenberg

SATURDAY
19

SUNDAY
20

(continued from page 82)

There are three trends in any market: the short-term, lasting from days to weeks; the intermediate, lasting from weeks to months; and the primary (long-term), lasting from months to years. The three trends are active all the time and can be moving in opposing directions.

The median extent of bear markets is a 29.4% decline from the previous bull market high, with 75% of all bear markets declining between 20.4% and 47.1%. The median duration of bear markets is 1.1 years, with 75% of all bear markets lasting between 0.8 and 2.8 years.

Of all the 694 corrections (secondary reactions) in history, 61% retraced between 30 and 70% of the previous primary swing, 65% lasted between three weeks and three months, and 98% lasted from two weeks to eight months. Minor reactions move in opposition to the intermediate trend and last less than two weeks 97.5% of the time. Sperandeo's conclusion: IF YOU KNOW WHAT THE TREND IS, AND YOU KNOW WHEN IT IS MOST LIKELY TO CHANGE, THEN YOU REALLY HAVE ALL THE KNOWLEDGE YOU NEED TO MAKE MONEY IN THE MARKETS.

The Trend Is Your Friend!

An uptrend is a price movement consisting of a series of higher highs and higher lows. A downtrend is a price movement consisting of lower lows and lower highs. These definitions apply to any market and to any time period.

A "line" is a price movement extending two to three weeks or longer, when the price variation moves within a range of 5% (like the 2850-3000 range which began in February 1991). Close observance on a daily basis is necessary to trade on the inevitable "break" to the downside or "breakout" on the upside.

It is important to note that volume in overbought markets becomes dull on rallies and increases on declines. In oversold markets, the tendency is for dullness on declines and activity on rallies. Bull markets begin on comparatively light volume and terminate during excessive activity.

A large number of market makers, floor traders and commodity traders try to ride the trend while watching resistance and support points—the previous highs and lows that make other "tide watchers" wary.

By watching the charts of the S&P 500 cash and S&P futures index, prudent speculators and investors can learn to recognize the pattern of program trading price movements and time their buys and sells to profit with the program traders.

To determine an uptrend, draw a line from below the lowest low, up and to the highest minor low point preceding the highest high, so that the line doesn't pass through prices between these two low points. Draw lines for downtrends above the highest high point to the lowest minor high point preceding the lowest low without passing through prices between these two points. This method, though simple, is extremely consistent and very accurate.

With practice you will learn to associate the three criteria of a change in a trend. 1) a break in the trend line; 2) a test of the preceding high or low; and 3) the breaking of a preceding minor rally high or selloff low. It's as easy as 1...2...3—the trend has changed.

(continued on page 85)

Daily Bar Chart

24000

22000

Sperandeo's 2B Rule. In an uptrend at point 2, if a higher high is made but fails to carry through, and prices dip below the previous high, the trend is apt to reverse. The converse is true for downtrends. This one observation alone has the greatest potential for catching the exact highs or lows, and is worth several hundred times the price of the book,

Understanding Moving Averages

A study done in 1968 by William Gordon showed that between 1917 and 1967 following Dow Theory would have returned an average yearly simple return of 18.1%, while buying and selling the Dow using the 200-day moving average would have returned 18.5% a year. This fact turned Sperandeo onto the 200-day, or 40-week moving average. (One large mutual fund advisory publication has successfully used only this indicator for years to get its people in or out of the market.)

If the 200-day moving average line flattens out following a previous decline or is advancing, and prices penetrate the moving average line on the upside, this comprises a major buy signal. If the 200-day moving average flattens out following a previous rise or is declining, and prices penetrate the line on the downside, a major sell is given. Sperandeo never buys a stock when prices are below this moving average, and he never sells a stock when the price is above it.

Another important Sperandeo tool is the relationship between the 10-week and 30-week moving averages. It's a buy when the 10-week crosses the 30-week and the slope of both averages is up. A sell signal is given on a crossover when the slopes of both are down.

FALL PORTFOLIO REVIEW

NO. OF SHARES	SECURITY	A ORIGINAL COST	B CURRENT VALUE	C GAIN (B-A) OR LOSS (A-B)	D % CHANGE (C ÷ A)	E MONTHS HELD	F CHANGE PER MO. (D ÷ E)	G ANNUAL RETURN (F×12)
200	Sample Corp.	$10,000	$10,400	$400	4.0%	8	0.5%	6.0%
TOTALS								

Stocks which have achieved their potential

1

2

3

Candidates for addition to portfolio

1

2

3

Stocks which have been disappointments

1

2

3

Investment decisions

1

2

3

SEPTEMBER

MONDAY
21

15.70 -.01   12.83 NC   27.50 +.04

If the aircraft industry had progressed as
rapidly as the semiconductor or computer
business in recent years, the Concorde
would now hold 10,000 passengers, travel
at 60,000 miles an hour and a ticket
would cost 1 cent.

TUESDAY
22

15.59 -.11   12.76 -.07   27.27 -.23

Don't try to buy at the bottom and sell
at the top. This can't be done —
except by liars.
— Bernard Baruch

WEDNESDAY
23

15.69 +.10   12.76 NC   27.23 -.04
Murphy @ Slota
R. Slota
+ review Phila @ Summary
2 Hrs ✓

A fall in price is followed on the
average by a further fall in price; a rise
in price by a further rise in price.
— Charles C. Ying (Computer Study)

THURSDAY
24

15.61 -.08   12.81 +.05   27.12 -.11

The best minds are not in government. If
any were, business would hire them away.
— Ronald Reagan

FRIDAY
25

1538 -.23   12.77 -.04   2691 -.21

$1,000 left to earn interest at 8% a year
will grow to $43 quadrillion in 400 years,
but the first hundred years are the hardest.
— Sidney Homer,
Salomon Brothers

SATURDAY
26

Birth, Growth, Maturity and
Murphy @ Slota
Prepare Phila returns for 1990, 91, 92   2 Hrs ✓
Computer Worksheet   2 Hrs ✓

SUNDAY
27

October, October don't show your face
Meltdown Monday '87 was a total disgrace

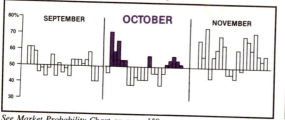

OCTOBER ALMANAC

See Market Probability Chart on page 159.

OCTOBER						
S	M	T	W	T	F	S
				1	2	3
4	5	6	7	8	9	10
11	12	13	14	15	16	17
18	19	20	21	22	23	24
25	26	27	28	29	30	31

NOVEMBER						
S	M	T	W	T	F	S
1	2	3	4	5	6	7
8	9	10	11	12	13	14
15	16	17	18	19	20	21
22	23	24	25	26	27	28
29	30					

☐ Curse of October 1929 was receding—then came 1987 and a 602-point loss in the Dow ☐ Memory of back-to-back "massacres" in 1978 and 1979, a "meltdown" in 1987 and Friday the Thirteenth in 1989 may affect bullish spirits in forthcoming Octobers ☐ October was known as a "bear-killer" having turned the tide in 6 major bear markets: 1946, 1957, 1960, 1962, 1966, and 1974 ☐ Third Friday expirations down 8 times, up a tad 5 times, in past 13 years ☐ A quiet anticipation month in election years, less than 1% change in 7 of last 9 elections.

OCTOBER DAILY POINT CHANGES DOW JONES INDUSTRIALS

Previous Month	1981	1982	1983	1984	1985	1986	1987	1988	1989	1990
Close	849.98	896.25	1233.13	1206.71	1328.63	1767.58	2596.28	2112.91	2692.82	2452.48
1	2.28	11.49	—	— 7.73	12.32	15.32	42.92	—	—	63.36
2	8.47	—	—	— 7.62	— 7.28	— 1.69	1.79	—	—	— 10.64
3	—	—	— 1.83	— 8.50	— 0.56	— 7.03	—	— 7.65	20.90	— 15.84
4	—	— 4.13	5.39	4.53	— 4.37	—	—	— 3.20	40.84	27.47
5	— 0.86	3.58	13.51	— 4.86	—	—	0.81	4.45	16.53	— 6.19
6	— 3.61	37.07	18.60	—	—	10.27	— 91.55	1.24	2.47	—
7	12.46	21.71	3.35	—	— 4.37	N/C	2.45	42.50	11.96	—
8	9.42	20.88	—	— 4.64	1.12	19.40	— 34.44	—	—	13.12
9	— 5.14	—	—	— 2.76	1.23	— 7.03	— 34.43	—	5.89	— 78.22
10	—	—	12.50	2.10	1.35	— 3.65	—	8.71	— 6.08	— 37.62
11	—	25.94	— 19.51	5.85	11.87	—	—	— 2.49	— 11.97	— 42.82
12	— 3.52	— 9.11	— 5.49	7.62	—	—	10.77	— 30.23	— 13.52	32.92
13	— 3.90	11.40	1.73	—	—	5.20	36.72	7.12	— 190.58	—
14	— 14.93	— 18.21	2.14	—	14.79	1.83	— 95.46	— 0.18	—	—
15	5.61	— 3.77	—	12.26	— 3.92	31.49	— 57.61	—	—	18.32
16	— 4.57	—	—	— 5.19	17.69	4.50	— 108.35	—	88.12	— 35.15
17	—	—	5.18	— 1.88	0.79	0.85	—	7.29	— 18.65	6.68
18	—	26.12	— 17.89	29.49	— 0.45	—	—	19.38	4.92	64.85
19	— 4.56	— 5.42	— 4.06	0.55	—	—	— 508.00	— 22.58	39.55	68.07
20	4.75	20.32	4.77	—	—	— 26.02	102.27	43.92	5.94	—
21	— 0.85	2.86	— 2.64	—	— 4.70	— 5.34	186.84	2.31	—	—
22	— 2.76	— 5.52	—	— 8.73	0.22	2.67	— 77.42	—	—	— 4.70
23	— 10.28	—	—	— 4.19	2.80	26.58	0.33	—	— 26.23	— 22.03
24	—	—	0.10	3.42	— 4.82	— 2.67	—	— 13.16	— 3.69	10.15
25	—	— 36.33	3.46	— 5.41	— 5.82	—	—	3.02	— 5.94	— 20.05
26	— 7.03	— 10.94	— 8.64	— 6.07	—	—	— 156.83	— 8.18	— 39.55	— 48.02
27	7.42	0.28	— 1.73	—	—	9.56	52.56	— 24.35	— 17.01	—
28	— 0.77	— 15.36	— 18.59	—	3.47	3.65	0.33	9.06	—	—
29	— 4.66	0.73	—	— 3.54	8.74	6.33	91.51	—	—	— 5.94
30	19.60	—	—	15.90	6.84	26.57	55.20	—	6.76	17.82
31	—	—	1.72	— 9.93	— 1.26	— 0.56	—	— 1.24	41.60	— 5.69
Close	852.55	991.72	1225.20	1207.38	1374.31	1877.81	1993.53	2148.65	2645.08	2442.33
Change	2.57	95.47	— 7.93	0.67	45.68	110.23	— 602.75	35.74	— 47.74	— 10.15

Rosh Hashana

MONDAY

28

15.38 NC 12.82 +.05 27.01 +.10

I always worry when bargains get hard
to find because historically that has
meant the market is fully valued
and will soon drop.
— W.J. Maeck

TUESDAY

29

15.55 +.17 12.84 +.02 27.08 +.07

Luck is the preparation for, recognition
of, and proper seizure of opportunity.
— Walter Heiby

WEDNESDAY

30

15.60 +.05 12.86 +.02 27.20 +.12

The Stock doesn't know you own it.
— "Adam Smith," *Money Game*

THURSDAY

1

15.31 — –.29 12.86 NC 27.14 –.06

Murphy's Law: Nothing is as easy as it
looks. Everything takes longer than you
think. If anything can go wrong, it will.

FRIDAY

2

15.15 –.16 12.76 –.10 26.84 –.30

The punishment of wise men who
refuse to take part in the affairs of
government is to live under the
government of unwise men.
— Plato

SATURDAY

3

SUNDAY

4

THE SEPTEMBER "REVERSE" BAROMETER

September always had special significance to Wall Streeters, as it was the start of a new business year. During the first sixty years of this century, the stock market in the final quarter of the year often took its cue from its own behavior in September and followed a similar course two-thirds of the time. As a result, September market activity was naturally regarded as a useful barometer and became folklore.

However, starting with 1960, an incredible transformation occurred. September became a **reverse barometer**. Bearish Septembers tended to be followed by bullish fourth quarters, and vice-versa. In the last 31 years, 21 Septembers were losers or gained less than 1.0%. They preceded average fourth quarter gains of 4.1%. Ten up Septembers preceded fourth quarters gaining 1.9%, on average.

AS SEPTEMBER GOES, BE CONTRARY!

Fourth-Quarter Performance

Year	1st Day in October	2nd Day in January	4th Quarter % Change
1960	53.36*	58.36*	9.4%
1961	66.77	71.13	6.5
1962	55.49	63.72	14.8
1963	72.22	75.50	4.5
1964	84.08	84.63	0.7
1965	89.90	92.26	2.6
1966	74.90	80.55	7.5
1967	96.32	95.67	− 0.7
1968	102.86	103.99	1.1
1969	92.52	93.46	1.0
1970	84.32	91.80	8.9
1971	98.93	102.09	3.2
1972	110.16	119.57	8.5
1973	108.21	99.80	− 7.8
1974	63.39	70.71	11.5
1975	82.93	92.58	11.6
1976	104.17	105.70	1.5
1977	96.74	93.52	− 3.3
1978	102.96	97.80	− 5.0
1979	108.56	105.22	− 3.1
1980	127.13	137.97	8.5
1981	117.08	120.05	2.5
1982	121.97	141.35	15.9
1983	165.80	166.78	0.6
1984	164.62	164.57	0.0
1985	185.07	210.88	13.9
1986	236.60	246.15	4.0
1987	327.33	255.94	−21.8
1988	271.38	279.43	3.0
1989	350.87	358.76	2.2
1990	314.94	321.91	2.2

*S & P Composite Index

Previous Septembers Bullish

Year	September %Change	4th Quarter %Change	Next Year's Change
1973	4.0%	− 7.8%	−29.7%
1988	4.0	3.0	27.3
1968	3.9	1.1	−11.4
1967	3.3	− 0.7	7.7
1970	3.3	8.9	10.8
1965	3.2	2.7	−13.1
1964	2.9	0.7	9.1
1980	2.5	8.5	− 9.7
1976	2.3	1.5	−11.5
1983	1.0	0.6	1.4
Averages	**3.0%**	**1.9%**	**− 1.9%**

Previous Septembers Bearish

Year	September %Change	4th Quarter %Change	Next Year's Change
1982	0.8%	15.9%	17.3%
1979	0.0	− 3.1	25.8
1977	− 0.2	− 3.3	1.1
1984	− 0.4	0.0	26.3
1972	− 0.5	8.5	−17.4
1978	− 0.7	− 5.0	12.3
1966	− 0.7	7.5	20.1
1971	− 0.7	3.2	15.6
1989	− 0.7	2.2	− 6.6
1963	− 1.1	4.5	13.0
1961	− 2.0	6.5	−11.8
1987	− 2.4	−21.8	12.4
1969	− 2.5	1.0	0.1
1985	− 3.5	13.9	14.6
1975	− 3.5	11.6	19.1
1962	− 4.8	14.8	18.9
1990	− 5.1	2.2	??
1981	− 5.4	2.5	14.8
1960	− 6.0	9.4	23.1
1986	− 8.5	4.0	2.0
1974	−11.9	11.5	31.5
Averages	**− 2.8%**	**4.1%**	**11.1%**

Even more incredible is September's record as a reverse barometer giving us advance notice of what the market will do in the following year. Six of the ten Septembers, with gains of 1.0% or more in Standard & Poor's composite index, were followed by bear market years (1974, 1969, 1966, 1981, 1977 and 1984 through August). The average loss was 1.9%. Twenty other Septembers were down, flat or slightly up and their following years gained 11.1% on average. Three losing years were not induced by recessions; 1962 (Kennedy stare-down with Big Steel and Cuban Missile Crisis), 1973 (OPEC oil embargo), and 1990 (Gulf Crisis).

OCTOBER

MONDAY
5

It is a socialist idea that making profits
is a vice; I consider the real vice
is making losses.
— Winston Churchill

TUESDAY
6

If you don't profit from your investment
mistakes, someone else will.
— Yale Hirsch

Yom Kippur

WEDNESDAY
7

The men who can manage men manage
the men who manage only things, and
the men who can manage money
manage all.
— Will Durant

THURSDAY
8

We make progress at night, while
the politicians sleep.
— Brazilian peasant proverb

FRIDAY
9

If all the economists in the world
were laid end to end, they still
wouldn't reach a conclusion.
— George Bernard Shaw

SATURDAY
10

SUNDAY
11

YEAR'S TOP INVESTMENT BOOKS

1. Trader Vic—Methods of a Wall Street Master, Victor Sperandeo, John Wiley & Sons, $24.95. Sperandeo integrates his knowledge of markets, technical analysis, odds and probability, fundamental analysis, economics, politics and human psychology and then reduces these elements to fundamental principles that you can profit from. Best Investment Book of the Year. See page 82.

2. Beating The Dow, Michael O'Higgins with John Downes, HarperCollins, $19.95. Investing in the five or ten Dow stocks paying the highest dividends the previous year could provide you with an exceptional return. Many more strategies for beating the Dow are featured. See page 16.

3. Classics—An Investor's Anthology, Edited by Charles D. Ellis with James R. Vertin, Dow Jones-Irwin, $39.95. A collection of some of the most enduring writing on investment theory and practice. Its five parts represent ideas and philosophies that have influenced investors over the last 60 years.

4. The 100 Best Stocks To Own In The World, Gene Walden, Dearborn Financial Publishing, $24.95. The 100 most outstanding companies in the world are profiled and rated according to six categories: earnings growth, stock growth, dividend yield, dividend growth, consistency and momentum.

5. Investing In Intangible Assets: Finding And Profiting From Hidden Corporate Value, Russell L. Parr. John Wiley & Sons, $34.95. Fills the gap that exists between understanding the financial performance of a company and understanding the hidden intangible assets which are a source of earnings and ultimately corporate value. This is the first book to clearly relate intangible assets to stock performance.

6. The Life And Times Of Dillon Read, Robert Sobel, E.P. Dutton, $24.95. The history of Dillon Read has mirrored the changing styles and practices of American finance. Noted business historian Robert Sobel presents an engrossing account of one of this nation's most prestigious financial institutions.

7. 101 Years On Wall Street: An Investor's Almanac, John Dennis Brown, Prentice Hall, $24.95 (paperback). Covers 101 years of market history, complete with charts, statistical information, market lore about big winners and losers and comparisons of all the bull and bear markets. Yearly retrospects provide analysis of how important news and practical events impact the market.

8. Complete Book Of Tax Deductions: 1991 Edition, Robert S. Holzman, Ph.D., HarperCollins, $14.95. The best book to consult for allowable tax deductions. Explains what steps you should take in order to prove your deductions. Helps set straight the confusion of our byzantine tax code.

9. Distressed Securities, Edward I. Altman, Probus Publishing, $50. The increased supply and variety of bankrupt and near-bankrupt companies, and the profit-making potential of securities selling at discounted prices, make distressed securities an attractive investment for the astute and aggressive investor. This is the first in-depth analysis of this market and its participants.

(continued on page 94)

OCTOBER

MONDAY

12

15.46 +.13   12.66 +.09   26.63 +.19

The trouble with government regulation
of the market is that it prohibits
capitalistic acts between
consenting adults.
— Professor Robert Nozick

TUESDAY

13

15.61 +.15   12.68 +.02   26.82 +.19   10.00 NC

In the final analysis, productivity is the
most important, most crucial thing for
the success of the new social order.
— Lenin

WEDNESDAY

14

Deflation to cure inflation is like
running over a man with a car and
then, to apologize, backing up and
running over him again.
— Sylvia Porter

THURSDAY

15

The actual course of the economy
depends mainly on the borrowing and
spending of consumers, businesses and
government units, the pricing policies
of business, the wage goals of labor,
and the tax laws of government.

FRIDAY

16

15.75

Money, which represents the prose of life,
and which is hardly spoken of in parlors
without an apology, is, in its effects
and laws as beautiful as roses.
— Ralph Waldo Emerson

SATURDAY

17

SUNDAY

18

(continued from page 92)

10. Investing With The Best, Claude N. Rosenberg, Jr., John Wiley & Sons, $24.95. What to look for and what to look out for in your search for a superior investment manager—whether you're responsible for a billion-dollar institutional portfolio or have several thousand dollars of personal funds to invest.

11. Convertible Bonds, Revised Edition, Thomas C. Noddings, Probus Publishing, $29.50. An introduction to a high-performance/low risk investment program using overlooked alternatives to traditional stocks, bonds and money market instruments. The variety of convertible bond investment strategies presented is designed to take full advantage of the low-risk, high-profit potential of these securities.

12. Outperforming Wall Street: Stock Market Profits Through Patience and Discipline, Second Edition, Daniel Alan Seiver, Prentice Hall, $27.95. The highly successful patience and discipline (PAD) strategy shows investors how to buy when stocks are cheap, sell when they are dear and select stocks that will outperform the market—in both bull and bear markets.

13. The RSL Market Timing System, Humphrey E. D. Lloyd, Windsor Books, $50. A powerful new timing method, designed to give investors the ability to call market turns as they occur. Tested for over 10 years in mutual funds, the method has produced profits on better than 4 out of 5 trades. More important, gains are more than 10 times larger than losses.

14. Stocks, Bonds, Bills, and Inflation Yearbook, Ibbotson Associates, $91. This annual reference book provides comprehensive total return data on all types of investments adjusted for risk and inflation since 1926. The premier source book for sales and research professionals.

When the market is blazing and investor interest is high, book publishers gobble up manuscripts on investing. But when stocks turn south and interest wanes, the demand for these manuscripts shrivels.

Last year's crop of books was huge and preceded the start of a bear market. It's ironic that there were fewer books to choose from this year as the Dow traveled sideways amid much skepticism about the bull market's durability. Fewer books may mean that the bull has longer to live.

Dearborn Financial Publishing
520 North Dearborn Street
Chicago IL 60610

Dow Jones-Irwin
1818 Ridge Road
Homewood IL 60430

E. P. Dutton
375 Hudson Street
New York NY 10014

HarperCollins Publishers
10 East 53rd Street
New York NY 10022

Ibbotson Associates
8 South Michigan
Suite 700
Chicago IL 60603

Prentice-Hall
Englewood Cliffs NJ 07632

Probus Publishing
1925 North Clybourn Street
Chicago IL 60606

John Wiley & Sons
605 Third Avenue
New York NY 10158

Windsor Books
Box 280
Brightwaters NY 11718

OCTOBER

15.99 +.24

If the volume has been decreasing for a
period of five consecutive trading days,
then there is a tendency for the price to
fall over the next four trading days.
— Charles C. Ying (Computer study)

16.01 +.02   12.75   27.30

A man may know what to do and lose
money if he doesn't do it quickly enough.
— Jesse Livermore

16.08 +.07   12.77   27.34 +.04

A cynic is a man who knows the price of
everything and the value of nothing.
— Oscar Wilde

16.10 +.02   12.76 -.01   27.19 - .15

There are three kinds of people or
companies: 1. those who make things
happen; 2. those who watch things
happen; and 3. those who ask,
"What happened?"

16.17 +.07   12.74 -.02   27.15 -.04

Chadwick Funeral Home - 1 hr ✓

Estate of Lillian A. Chadwick

Review assets, checkbook, etc.   3hrs

There are old traders around and
bold traders around but there are
no old, bold traders around.
— Bob Dinda, Dean Witter

MARKET "VOTES" FOR REPUBLICANS IN NOVEMBER

Since 1900, the market has shown an obvious preference for Republican presidents by rising the following day on ten of the thirteen occasions a Republican has won the election (average change +0.89%) and on only three of the ten occasions a Democrat has won (average change −0.77%). The week and month following Republican victories saw gains of 1.48% and 2.49%; losses of 0.61% and 2.06% followed Democratic victories. As the market was open on Election Day in 1984 for the first time and the outcome was a foregone conclusion, I included that day's results instead of those of the day after (also in 1988).

MONTHLY % CHANGES DURING ELECTION YEARS **

Year	JAN	FEB	MAR	APR	MAY	JUN	JUL	AUG	SEP	OCT	NOV	DEC
1900	0.1	− 3.3	3.2	− 7.1	− 3.6	− 7.1	3.4	1.8	− 6.1	8.8	12.8	6.2
1904	− 0.4	− 2.8	3.3	− 0.7	− 1.3	2.2	5.8	4.7	5.5	9.4	14.2	− 3.3
1908	6.7	− 3.4	11.5	3.0	4.6	− 0.2	10.7	5.4	− 5.6	3.3	5.8	− 1.3
1912	− 1.8	1.5	8.4	2.3	− 2.5	3.3	− 1.3	2.1	2.8	− 3.7	0.8	− 3.9
1916	− 8.6	− 4.1	4.2	− 2.3	4.5	− 2.4	− 4.3	− 9.1	0.5	2.5	− 2.5	2.4
1920	− 3.8	−12.0	12.6	− 9.0	− 1.6	− 1.4	− 4.3	− 0.8	− 3.7	2.4	−10.5	− 5.4
1924	5.4	− 3.4	− 4.3	− 2.6	− 0.8	7.2	6.0	3.0	− 1.9	0.9	7.0	8.2
1928	− 1.9	− 1.9	9.5	− 0.8	3.9	− 4.2	2.6	11.3	− 0.4	5.3	− 5.1	2.2
1932	− 2.8	5.0	−11.8	−20.2	−23.3	− 0.9	37.7	37.5	− 3.7	−13.9	− 5.9	5.2
1936	6.6	1.7	2.5	− 7.7	4.6	3.1	6.8	0.9	0.1	7.5	0.4	− 0.6
1940	− 3.5	0.7	1.0	− 0.5	−24.0	7.7	3.1	2.6	0.9	3.9	− 4.2	− 0.3
1944	1.5	− 0.2	1.7	− 1.2	4.0	5.1	− 2.1	0.9	− 0.3	N/C	0.4	3.5
1948	− 4.0	− 4.7	7.7	2.7	7.8	0.3	− 5.3	0.8	− 3.0	6.8	−10.8	3.1
1952	1.6	− 3.6	4.8	− 4.3	2.3	4.6	1.8	− 1.5	− 2.0	− 0.1	4.6	3.5
1956	− 3.6	3.5	6.9	− 0.2	− 6.6	3.9	5.2	− 3.8	− 4.5	0.5	− 1.1	3.5
1960	− 7.1	0.9	− 1.4	− 1.8	2.7	2.0	− 2.5	2.6	− 6.0	− 0.2	4.0	4.6
1964	2.7	1.0	1.5	0.6	1.1	1.6	1.8	− 1.6	2.9	0.8	− 0.5	0.4
1968	− 4.4	− 3.1	0.9	8.2	1.1	0.9	− 1.8	1.1	3.9	0.7	4.8	− 4.2
1972	1.8	2.5	0.6	0.4	1.7	− 2.2	0.2	3.4	− 0.5	0.9	4.6	1.2
1976	11.8	− 1.1	3.1	− 1.1	− 1.4	4.1	− 0.8	− 0.5	2.3	− 2.2	− 0.8	5.2
1980	5.8	− 0.4	−10.2	4.1	4.7	2.7	6.5	0.6	2.5	1.6	10.2	− 3.4
1984	− 0.9	− 3.9	1.3	0.5	− 6.0	1.7	− 1.6	10.6	− 0.4	− 0.0	− 2.0	2.2
1988	4.0	4.2	− 3.3	0.9	0.3	4.3	− 0.5	− 3.9	4.0	2.6	− 1.9	1.5
Totals*	8.0	−31.9	65.5	−16.6	19.5	37.2	29.4	30.6	− 9.0	51.7	30.2	25.3
Up	11	9	18	9	13	16	13	16	10	17	12	15
Down	12	14	5	14	10	7	10	7	13	6	11	8

*Excludes 1932 and May 1940   **Dow Jones industrials 1900-1928
                                        S&P composite since 1932

The market's monthly percent changes for all the election years since 1900 reveals much of our history, such as the Depression's roller coaster market in 1932, or the fall of France in May 1940. The market's best performing month was March: up 18, down 5. The two double-digit losses were during the Depression and the Hunt/Silver crisis in 1980. Some other observations: January has been the most volatile month; February, April and September have the worst records; in March, April, May and June, markets have been upbeat in recent years; July and August are the convention months; September has been the election bear month as campaigns kick off; October is the least volatile month as we await the election; and November is a swing month, usually up sharply when Republicans are victorious. Second halves (up 208.74%), were stronger than first halves (down 1.3%). Excluding all of 1932 and May 1940 changes the figures to +151.7% vs. +76.7%.

16.21 +.04   12.80 +.06   27.40 +.25

MONDAY

26

Capital formation is shifting from the
entrepreneur who invests in the future to
the pension trustee who invests in the past.
— Peter Drucker

16.25 +.04   12.81 +.01   27.42 +.02

TUESDAY

27

In order to be a great writer a person must
have a built-in, shockproof crap detector.
— Ernest Hemingway
(Ed. Try substituting the word
"investor" for "writer.")

16.43 +.18   12.84 +.03 27.57 +.15

WEDNESDAY

28

All the perplexities, confusion and distress
in America arise, not from the defects in
their constitution or confederation...
as from downright ignorance of the
nature of coin, credit and circulation.
— John Q. Adams

.15 16.52 +.09   12.86 +.02   27.69 +.12

THURSDAY

29

Don't be overly concerned about your
heirs. Usually, unearned funds do
them more harm than good.
— Gerald M. Loeb

.23 16.50 −.02   12.82 −.04   27.61 −.08

FRIDAY

30

Chadwick Funeral Home
Pension Plan —
Notice @ SPD

Risk is actually lowest when people see it
as the greatest, and when most people
think of it as absent, it is actually
the highest.
— Dick A. Stoken
(Strategic Investment Timing, 1984)

SATURDAY

31

SUNDAY

1

Two days pre-Thanksgiving, one day more
A rally we all can be thankful for

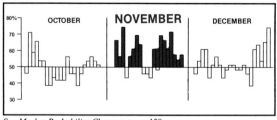

See Market Probability Chart on page 159.

NOVEMBER ALMANAC

NOVEMBER							DECEMBER					
S	M	T	W	T	F	S	S	M	T	W	T	F	S
1	2	3	4	5	6	7				1	2	3	4	5
8	9	10	11	12	13	14	6	7	8	9	10	11	12
15	16	17	18	19	20	21	13	14	15	16	17	18	19
22	23	24	25	26	27	28	20	21	22	23	24	25	26
29	30						27	28	29	30	31	

☐ Best percentage gainer in 41 years based on S&P composite index, up an average 1.7% per year ☐ Up 27 times, down 14, but only 3 losses over 2.0% (1969, −3.5%; 1973, −11.4%; and 1974, −5.3%) until 1987's huge −8.5% ☐ Day before and day after Thanksgiving combined 21 years without a loss until 1987 (pg. 102) ☐ Anticipators have pushed up preceding Tuesday 7 years in a row until 1990 ☐ November, December and January comprise best 3 months of the year ☐ Five second-term re-election victories were followed by four healthy bear markets.

NOVEMBER DAILY POINT CHANGES DOW JONES INDUSTRIALS

	1981	1982	1983	1984	1985	1986	1987	1988	1989	1990
Previous Month Close	852.55	991.72	1225.20	1207.38	1374.31	1877.81	1993.53	2148.65	2645.08	2442.33
1	—	13.98	4.07	9.71	15.94	—	—	2.31	0.82	12.62
2	14.27	16.38	8.03	− 0.44	—	—	20.56	5.87	−14.34	35.89
3	1.90	43.41	−10.17	—	—	16.45	−50.56	13.51	− 2.05	—
4	− 1.90	−15.27	− 8.84	—	− 0.57	− 1.82	−18.24	−24.54	—	—
5	− 7.71	1.56	—	12.59	6.99	6.60	40.12	—	—	11.39
6	− 6.66	—	—	14.91	6.77	− 7.45	−26.36	—	−47.34	−17.08
7	—	—	− 3.45	−10.93	− 3.90	− 5.06	—	−21.16	14.96	−44.31
8	—	−14.34	0.10	− 4.53	4.82	—	—	2.85	26.23	2.97
9	2.76	22.81	17.58	− 9.72	—	—	−58.85	− 9.25	−19.67	44.80
10	− 1.23	−15.73	3.35	—	—	5.76	−22.05	− 3.55	21.92	—
11	3.14	10.21	14.33	—	27.52	3.66	21.05	−47.66	—	—
12	3.42	−14.81	—	0.22	1.72	− 2.25	61.01	—	—	51.74
13	− 4.66	—	—	−12.59	− 5.85	−31.50	−25.20	—	0.82	− 4.95
14	—	—	3.87	0.33	11.47	11.39	—	− 1.95	−16.18	24.25
15	—	−18.49	− 6.10	− 0.77	− 4.13	—	—	12.09	22.33	−14.60
16	−10.85	−13.43	3.35	−18.22	—	—	14.09	−38.59	3.08	5.20
17	5.14	19.50	3.35	—	—	−13.07	−26.85	13.87	17.00	—
18	− 6.09	4.60	− 3.65	—	4.93	−43.31	16.91	9.96	—	—
19	0.67	−10.85	—	− 2.65	− 1.03	9.42	−43.77	—	—	15.10
20	8.18	—	—	9.83	0.23	34.03	18.24	—	−20.62	−35.15
21	—	—	17.78	6.40	23.05	32.90	—	3.56	7.25	9.16
22	—	−21.25	7.01	H	2.06	—	—	11.73	17.49	H
23	− 1.14	− 9.01	− 0.20	18.78	—	—	9.45	14.58	H	−12.13
24	18.45	9.01	H	—	—	12.51	40.45	H	18.77	—
25	7.90	H	1.83	—	− 7.68	6.05	−16.58	−17.60	—	—
26	H	7.36	—	− 7.95	0.12	4.64	H	—	—	5.94
27	7.80	—	—	7.84	18.92	H	−36.47	—	19.42	10.64
28	—	—	− 7.62	−14.80	H	− 2.53	—	6.76	7.04	− 8.66
29	—	− 4.51	17.38	−11.93	− 3.56	—	—	20.09	−13.23	−16.34
30	3.04	36.43	−11.18	− 4.52	—	—	−76.93	12.98	17.49	40.84
Close	888.98	1039.28	1276.02	1188.94	1472.13	1914.23	1833.55	2114.51	2706.27	2559.65
Change	36.43	47.56	50.82	−18.44	97.82	36.42	−159.98	−34.14	61.19	117.32

12.89   27.57

NOVEMBER

2

LILLIAN CHADWICK, ESTATE
F10 976.69
16.28   16.51±.01   12877.05 27.79 +.18
16.51±.01

Institutions tend to dump stock in a single
transaction and buy, if possible, in smaller
lots, gradually accumulating a position.
Therefore, many more big blocks are
traded on downticks than on upticks.
— Justin Mamis

16.32

Election Day   **TUESDAY**

3

16.46 -.05   12.84 -.03   27.69 -.10

Among the portfolio managers of giant
insurance companies, bank trust
departments and mutual funds, I have
found that market know-how decreases
as surroundings become more plush.
— William A. Kent

16.37

WEDNESDAY

4

Chadwick Funeral H
16.50 +.04   12.79 -.05   27.54 -.15

2 1/2 Hours
Plowing Estate
11 1/2 · 11 1/2   1 1/2

The worst crime against working people is a
company that fails to make a profit.
— Samuel Gompers

Estate of Lillian A. Chadwick — Inc
16.43   Inheritance — Tax
16.73 +.23   12.83 +.04   27.63 +.09

THURSDAY

5

Stocks are sometimes the strongest when
they look the weakest, and the weakest
when they look the strongest.
— Peter Wyckoff

16.50   16.86 +.13   12.82 -.01   27.67 +.04

FRIDAY

6

For every dollar reaching the needy, the
cost of channeling it through churches is
8 cents; through charitable organizations,
27 cents — and to get one dollar
through government, it costs $3.00!
— Gary Allen

SATURDAY

7

SUNDAY

8

PREDICT WINNER OF 1992 ELECTION
WITH YEAR-EARLIER INTEREST RATE LEVEL

Television newscasters often predict election results by polling voters leaving voting booths. This practice has incurred the wrath of many citizens who feel that people who haven't voted yet may be influenced and thus decide not to vote.

Announcing victors hours before the final votes are cast might violate the spirit of democracy, but what if a simple statistic could tell election results a year in advance?

Knowing AAA Corporate bond yields would have enabled you to foretell the outcome of each presidential election since 1920—one year in advance. Dick A. Stoken* discovered that when the level of long-term interest rates was relatively high one year prior to the election, the party in power was ousted one year later. This phenomenon was at work in the elections of Harding (1920), Roosevelt (1932), Eisenhower (1952), Kennedy (1960), Nixon (1968), Carter (1976) and Reagan (1980).

When long-term rates fall to a fifteen-month low, a period of "low" interest rates begins which remains until rates climb again to a seven-year high. The other nine presidents in the table were all fortunate to have run during a period of low interest rates, enabling their parties to hold onto the White House for an additional four years.

Interest rates of 15.85% in October 1981 fell to 12.42% in November 1983, one year prior to the 1984 election. Gallup and Harris...move over!

Rates on AAAs fell to 7.42% by April 1986 and remained fairly stable for a year. They then rose swiftly during the spring of 1987 reaching 9.10% by May. The prime rate simultaneously moved up from 7½% to 8¼%. Rates at these levels on November 15 made it more expensive for millions of Americans to finance new homes and new cars and expand their businesses. This discomfort should have translated into a loss of the White House by the Republicans in 1988. But the Democrats blew it when their candidate turned out to be inept.

*Strategic Investment Timing, Probus

INTEREST RATES ONE YEAR PRIOR TO PRESIDENTIAL ELECTIONS

Election	Interest Rates November 15 1 Year Earlier	Incumbent Party	Popular Vote %	Challenging Party	Popular Vote %	Plurality
1920	High	Cox (D)	34.1	Harding (R)	60.4	26.3%
1924	Low	Coolidge (R)	54.0	Davis (D)[a]	28.2	25.8%
1928	Low	Hoover (R)	58.1	Smith (D)	40.8	17.3%
1932	High	Hoover (R)	39.7	Roosevelt (D)	57.4	17.7%
1936	Low	Roosevelt (D)	60.8	Landon (D)	36.5	24.3%
1940	Low	Roosevelt (D)	54.7	Wilkie (R)	44.8	9.9%
1944	Low	Roosevelt (D)	53.4	Dewey (R)	45.9	7.5%
1948	Low	Truman (D)	49.6	Dewey (R)[b]	45.1	4.5%
1952	High	Stevenson (D)	44.4	Eisenhower (R)	55.1	10.7%
1956	Low	Eisenhower (R)	57.4	Stevenson (D)	42.0	15.4%
1960	High	Nixon (R)	49.5	Kennedy (D)	49.7	0.2%
1964	Low	Johnson (D)	61.1	Goldwater (R)	38.5	22.6%
1968	High	Humphrey (D)	42.7	Nixon (R)[c]	43.4	0.7%
1972	Low	Nixon (R)	60.7	McGovern (D)	37.5	23.2%
1976	High	Ford (R)	48.3	Carter (D)	50.4	2.1%
1980	High	Carter (D)	41.9	Reagan (R)	51.8	9.9%
1984	Low	Reagan (R)	59.1	Mondale (D)	40.9	18.2%
1988	High	Bush (R)	53.9	Dukakis (D)	46.1	7.8%

Winners in italics, a) LaFollette (Progressive) 16%, b) Thurmond and Henry Wallace combined 5%, c) Geo. Wallace 13%

NOVEMBER

MONDAY

9

15.75   12.89   27.57

16.57 16.92 +.06   12.84 .02 27.74 +.07

A generation which ignores history
has no past — and no future.
— Robert A. Heinlein

TUESDAY

10

16.65   17.06 +.14   12.87 +.03   27.81 +.07

New issues: The closest thing to a "Sure
Thing" Wall Street has to offer.
— Norm Fosback, *New Issues*

Veteran's Day

WEDNESDAY

11

6.72   17.17 +.11   12.93 +.06 27.99 +.18

Don't confuse brains with a bull market.
— Humphrey Neill

THURSDAY

12

.79   17.21 +.04   12.96 +.03   28.03 +.04

Business has only two functions
—marketing and innovation.
— Peter Drucker

FRIDAY

13

.96   17.20 -.01   12.94 -.02 28.06 +.03

If I owe a million dollars I am lost. But if
I owe $50 billion the bankers are lost.
— Celso Ming

SATURDAY

14

SUNDAY

15

THANKSGIVING MARKET–NO TURKEY!
SURE WAY TO WIN THE TURKEY SHOOT

Easy! Be invested on the day before and after Thanksgiving. These two days combined gained about nine Dow points on average for 21 straight years without a loss until 1987's crash. In 39 years there were only five losses. Thanksgiving strength may be attributed to the Holiday spirit, but the month of November has been the Number One percentage gainer since 1950 (S&P 500). I would go long prior to the Wednesday before Thanksgiving. As 13 of the following Mondays in the past 19 years were losers, I would tend to exit early on the Friday after Thanksgiving, if Wednesday had a good gain. However, notice in recent years Tuesdays were up thanks to anticipators and four Fridays in a row were down because of an early exodus.

WHAT DOW JONES INDUSTRIALS DID ON
THE DAY BEFORE AND AFTER THANKSGIVING

	2 Days Before	Day Before	Day After	Total Gain Dow Points	Dow Close	Next Monday
1952		1.54	1.22	2.76	283.66	0.04
1953		0.65	2.45	3.10	280.23	1.14
1954		1.89	3.16	5.05	387.79	0.72
1955		0.71	0.26	0.97	482.88	− 1.92
1956		− 2.16	4.65	2.49	472.36	− 2.27
1957		10.69	3.84	14.53	449.87	− 2.96
1958		8.63	8.31	16.94	557.46	2.61
1959		1.41	1.42	2.83	652.52	6.66
1960		1.37	4.00	5.37	606.47	− 1.04
1961		1.10	2.18	3.28	732.60	− 0.61
1962		4.31	7.62	11.93	644.87	− 2.81
1963		− 2.52	9.52	7.00	750.52	1.39
1964		− 5.21	− 0.28	− 5.49	882.12	− 6.69
1965		n/c	− 0.78	− 0.78	948.16	− 1.23
1966		1.84	6.52	8.36	803.34	− 2.18
1967		3.07	3.58	6.65	877.60	4.51
1968		− 3.17	8.76	5.59	985.08	− 1.74
1969		3.23	1.78	5.01	812.30	− 7.26
1970		1.98	6.64	8.62	781.35	12.74
1971		0.66	17.96	18.62	816.59	13.14
1972		7.29	4.67	11.96	1025.21	− 7.45
1973		10.08	− 0.98	9.10	854.00	−29.05
1974		2.03	− 0.63	1.40	618.66	−15.64
1975		3.15	2.12	5.27	860.67	− 4.33
1976		1.66	5.66	7.32	956.62	− 6.57
1977		0.78	1.12	1.90	844.42	− 4.85
1978		2.95	3.12	6.07	810.12	3.72
1979		− 1.80	4.35	2.55	811.77	16.98
1980		7.00	3.66	10.66	993.34	−23.69
1981		7.90	7.80	15.70	885.94	3.04
1982		9.01	7.36	16.37	1007.36	− 4.51
1983	7.01	− 0.20	1.83	1.63	1277.44	− 7.62
1984	9.83	6.40	18.78	25.18	1220.30	− 7.95
1985	0.12	18.92	− 3.56	15.36	1472.13	−14.22
1986	6.05	4.64	− 2.53	2.11	1914.23	− 1.55
1987	40.45	−16.58	−36.47	−53.05	1910.48	−76.93
1988	11.73	14.58	−17.60	− 3.02	2074.68	6.76
1989	7.25	17.49	18.77	36.26	2675.55	19.42
1990	−35.15	9.16	−12.13	− 2.97	2527.33	5.94

15.75   12.89   27.57

NOVEMBER

MONDAY

.93   17.14 -.06   12.91 -.03   27.93 -.13

16

Always listen to experts. They'll tell you
what can't be done, and why.
Then do it!
— Robert A. Heinlein

PA INHERITANCE TAX — ESTATE OF L. CHADWICK

TUESDAY

.97

16.95 -.19   12.89 -.02   27.83 -.10

INCOME TAX INSTITUTE

SOUDERTON

17

What, sir, you would make a ship sail
against the wind and currents by lighting
a bonfire under her decks? I pray you
to excuse me. I have no time to listen
to such nonsense.
— Napoleon to Robert Fulton

17.04   17.19 +.24   12.96 +.07   28.08 +.25

WEDNESDAY

INCOME TAX INSTITUTE

SOUDERTON

Murphy & Slota — Phila Wage Taxes Processing

5 Hours ✓

18

The Fed is not immune to political
pressures, as its refusal to up its discount
rate before the election, and its well-
publicized crackdown on prime
rates after, amply demonstrates.
— M.S. Forbes, Jr.

INCOME TAX INSTITUTE

WORGANTOWN

THURSDAY

17.09   17.35 +.16   12.97 +.01   28.25 +.17

19

The advancement of the arts from year to
year taxes our credulity and seems to
presage the arrival of that period when
further improvement must end.
— Henry L. Ellsworth, U.S.
Commissioner of Patents, 1844

MORGANTOWN

FRIDAY

.15

INCOME TAX INSTITUTE

17.37 +.02   13.00 +.03   28.40 +.15

☠ # 20

The extraordinary increase in technical
indicators will tend to improve the
status of a non-technician.
— Humphrey Neill

SATURDAY

21

SUNDAY

22

"JANUARY EFFECT" FAVORS SMALL STOCKS BUT JUDGE THE RESULTS FOR YOURSELF

My research on the January Effect since 1953 using the S&P Low-Priced stock index as a proxy for small stocks vs. the blue-chip S&P 500 is shown in the table.

Simply stated, the January Effect is the tendency for small stocks to outperform large stocks in January. Hundreds have studied this effect. Two professors, Robert A Haugen and Josef Lakonichok, analyzed all the research and wrote "The Incredible January Effect" (Dow Jones-Irwin).

Some of their conclusions:

* Average returns to the stocks of small companies in January are typically larger than those of the biggest companies.

* In January buying the Value Line index futures contract while selling the S&P 500 contract is a profitable hedge strategy.

* Low-grade bonds beat higher-grade bonds and non-dividend paying stocks outperform the dividend payers in January.

* The January Effect has been in operation since the introduction of the income tax and it's even more prevalent in foreign countries.

Low-priced stocks had double-digit gains and a better "batting average" than the S&P 500 in 1961, 1968, 1971, 1972, 1974, 1975, 1976, 1979 and 1991. These were Januarys following bear markets or when the stock market was clobbered late in the year.

Though the low-priced stock index outperformed the S&P 500 in 36 out of the past 39 Januarys by 5.5 percentage points on average, note that the margin between the two has been smaller in recent years until 1991.

January losses for low-priced stocks resulted in 1969, 1973, 1978, 1982, and 1990 when bear markets began or were in progress, at least for the smaller capitalization issues.

Prospects for January 1992 are good as low-priced stocks have been up in every election year in the last four decades and have also outperformed the market.

JANUARY % CHANGES
(Based on Monthly Averages)

	Daily S&P 500 Index	Weekly Low-Priced Index	Difference
1953	0.5%	4.6%	4.1%
1954	2.5	7.6	5.1
1955	1.8	7.8	6.0
1956	−2.7	0.9	3.6
1957	−2.2	·4.0	6.2
1958	2.0	8.7	6.7
1959	4.0	6.9	2.9
1960	−1.7	3.1	4.8
1961	5.1	·10.0	4.9
1962	−3.7	2.2	5.9
1963	3.9	4.8	0.9
1964	3.1	5.7	2.6
1965	2.6	· 6.1	3.5
1966	1.7	3.2	1.5
1967	3.8	7.1	3.3
1968	−0.3	15.1	15.4
1969	−4.2	−4.7	− 0.5
1970	−8.7	3.7	12.4
1971	3.3	14.4	11.1
1972	4.2	13.1	8.9
1973	0.8	− 3.6	− 4.4
1974	1.4	14.7	13.3
1975	8.2	28.5	20.3
1976	9.2	16.8	7.6
1977	−0.9	· 6.3	7.2
1978	−3.8	− 1.4	2.4
1979	3.7	11.9	8.2
1980	3.5	7.3	3.8
1981	−0.4	2.9	3.3
1982	−5.3	− 0.3	5.0
1983	3.5	6.1	2.6
1984	1.2	4.7	3.5
1985	4.3	· 9.0	4.7
1986	0.4	1.9	1.5
1987	6.4	8.4	2.0
1988	4.0	7.1	3.1
1989	3.2	· 7.4	4.2
1990	−2.5	−3.8	−1.3
1991	4.2*	21.0*	16.8
39-year Average	**1.4%**	**6.9%**	**5.5%**

*Month-end prices now available

Johnson− (at 1965)

Carter (at 1977)

(handwritten annotations beside 1957, 1961, 1973, 1981)

* Two years after election

104

NOVEMBER

MONDAY
23

17.19 Ph. 12. Textile - bowrer Auctorwur
PFP Seminar - 8:00AM
17.24 -.13   12.99 -.01   28.29 -.11

The population of the earth decreases
every day, and, if this continues, in
another 10 centuries the earth
will be nothing but a desert.
— Montesquieu, 1743

TUESDAY
24

17.22   17.37 +.13   13.03 +.04   28.47 +.18

Any stock in too many institutional
portfolios or the subject of excess
advisory bullishness should be
suspect. Someday a majority
will want to take profits.
— Gerald M. Loeb

WEDNESDAY
25

17.24   17.38 +.01   13.09 +.06   28.56 +.09

If you buy one man's vote, it's a felony.
If you buy millions of votes at one time,
it's Congressional or Presidential
campaign strategy.
— Richard Russell

**Thanksgiving
(Market Closed)**

THURSDAY
26

The first thing a person does when he
discovers something which may alter the
value of certain securities, is not to
print it on a news ticker but to buy or
sell the stock himself, and then tell
his friends about it.
— Richard D. Wyckoff

FRIDAY
27

17.28   17.38 N C   13.10 +.01   28.62 +.06

Don't gamble! Take all savings and buy
some good stock and hold it till it goes up,
then sell it. If it don't go up, don't buy it.
— Will Rogers

SATURDAY
28

SUNDAY
29

If Santa Claus should fail to call
Bears may come to Broad and Wall

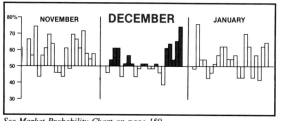

DECEMBER ALMANAC

See Market Probability Chart on page 159.

DECEMBER						
S	M	T	W	T	F	S
		1	2	3	4	5
6	7	8	9	10	11	12
13	14	15	16	17	18	19
20	21	22	23	24	25	26
27	28	29	30	31		

JANUARY						
S	M	T	W	T	F	S
					1	2
3	4	5	6	7	8	9
10	11	12	13	14	15	16
17	18	19	20	21	22	23
24	25	26	27	28	29	30
31						

□ "Free lunch" served on Wall Street at mid-month (pg. 108) □ Low-priced stocks usually beat high quality in January □ Gold great buy in fourth quarters (pg. 80) □ RECORD: S&P up 30, down 11 □ December is second best month, with average 1.6% gain and second with 650.72 total Dow points gained since 1950 □ Big 105 Dow points gained in 1987, after the crash. □ For January Effect see page 104 □ Since 1950 pre-election Decembers usually up sharply, 4.2% on average.

DECEMBER DAILY POINT CHANGES DOW JONES INDUSTRIALS

	1981	1982	1983	1984	1985	1986	1987	1988	1989	1990
Previous Month Close	888.98	1039.28	1276.02	1188.94	1472.13	1914.23	1833.55	2114.51	2706.27	2559.65
1	1.24	− 8.19	− 0.92	—	—	− 1.55	8.79	−12.63	41.38	—
2	− 7.61	2.02	− 9.86	—	−14.22	−42.89	6.63	− 9.60	—	—
3	1.24	− 1.75	—	− 6.52	1.15	− 8.30	−72.44	—	—	5.94
4	8.84	—	—	2.65	25.34	7.59	− 9.79	—	5.98	14.11
5	—	—	5.29	−13.47	− 1.49	−14.62	—	31.48	−11.95	30.70
6	—	24.29	− 1.22	− 1.11	− 5.73	—	—	25.60	− 4.91	− 7.92
7	− 5.70	1.29	4.47	− 7.28	—	—	45.43	4.27	−15.99	−12.38
8	− 5.24	− 9.85	−11.89	—	—	5.20	56.20	−11.92	10.66	—
9	6.47	−19.13	1.83	—	19.84	−13.36	34.15	1.78	—	—
10	3.81	− 9.20	—	9.05	2.18	16.03	−47.08	—	—	6.68
11	− 5.52	—	—	6.07	12.50	− 9.28	11.60	—	− 3.20	−10.64
12	—	—	1.53	− 3.20	− 0.46	−11.39	—	− 3.91	23.89	36.14
13	—	5.52	− 5.70	− 6.29	23.97	—	—	− 3.91	8.96	− 7.92
14	−15.03	−14.90	− 9.24	7.07	—	—	65.82	− 9.24	− 7.46	−20.55
15	4.47	−16.74	− 9.86	—	—	10.55	8.62	− 1.25	−14.08	—
16	− 7.23	− 2.39	5.38	—	17.89	13.35	32.99	17.71	—	—
17	1.81	21.25	—	0.88	− 8.60	−17.85	−50.07	—	—	− 0.49
18	5.23	—	—	34.78	− 2.07	5.49	50.90	—	−42.02	33.41
19	—	—	2.44	− 3.53	1.49	16.03	—	21.97	− 1.92	N/C
20	—	6.99	− 2.64	− 4.75	− 0.92	—	—	− 6.61	− 7.68	2.73
21	− 2.66	25.75	13.01	− 4.31	—	—	15.08	− 1.43	3.20	4.20
22	− 1.14	4.78	− 1.32	—	—	2.67	−11.93	− 4.28	20.26	—
23	− 2.29	10.03	− 3.15	—	−14.22	−11.81	27.19	8.57	—	—
24	3.71	—	—	11.16	− 9.63	12.51	− 5.97	—	—	−12.37
25	H	H	H	H	H	H	H	H	H	H
26	—	—	—	1.22	7.34	3.52	—	—	− 2.13	15.84
27	—	25.48	13.21	6.40	16.51	—	—	− 6.25	15.14	−11.63
28	− 3.04	−11.68	− 0.51	1.65	—	—	−56.70	3.75	7.90	3.71
29	− 2.09	0.73	− 3.05	—	—	−18.28	−16.08	16.25	20.90	—
30	4.85	−12.23	− 1.52	—	7.46	− 3.51	23.21	−14.11	—	—
31	1.90	− 0.83	—	7.40	− 3.79	−12.66	−11.27	—	—	4.45
Close	875.00	1046.54	1258.64	1211.57	1546.67	1895.95	1938.83	2168.57	2753.20	2633.66
Change	−13.98	7.26	−17.38	22.63	74.54	−18.28	105.28	54.06	46.93	74.01

√GTCY VTRSX VRYCC

NOV/DECEMBER

MONDAY 30

DO SUMMARY PLAN DESCRIPTIONS FOR
14.30 / 16.80   17.89 +.21   13.11+.01   28.70 +.08
MURPHY & SLOTA
~~CHADWICK FUNERAL HOME~~
ARDMORE BEVERAGE -

TUESDAY 1

~~ORDER SUBSCRIPTION TO OTC STOCKS~~
17.36 / 16.85   17.73+.14   13.13+.02   28.91 +.01

Murphy & Slota - Profit Sharing Plan
Allocations SAR, SAR (15)
& Revisions   8 Hrs

WEDNESDAY 2

17.43   17.70 -.03 13.12 -.01 28.64 -.07

Murphy & Slota — Profit Sharing plan
Proofing, and assembly, delivery
                    11½ Hrs

THURSDAY 3

17.48   17.76 +.06 13.12 NC 28.65 +.01

FRIDAY 4

17.54   17.91 +.15 13.17 +.05 28.76 +.11

SATURDAY 5

11:00 AM R Chadwick - C. Chadwick   1½ hr

SUNDAY 6

MID-DECEMBER NEW LOWS
THE ONLY FREE LUNCH ON WALL STREET

Several shrewd observers have noted that many depressed issues sell at "bargain" levels near the close of each year as investors rid their portfolios of these "losers" for tax purposes. This was first featured in 1970. Stocks hitting new lows for the year around December 15 in 1966, 1967, and 1968 outperformed the market handsomely by February 15 in the following year.

BARGAIN STOCKS VS. THE MARKET

Period of Dec. 15-Feb. 15	No. of New Lows Around Dec. 15	% Change by Feb.15	% Change in NYSE Composite	Net Gain
1966-67	45	18.0%	8.9%	9.1%
1967-68	45	7.4	— 4.7	12.1
1968-69	24	5.0	— 3.4	8.4
1974-75	112	48.9	22.1	26.8
1975-76	21	34.9	14.9	20.0
1976-77	②)	1.3	— 3.3	4.6
1977-78	15	2.8	— 4.5	7.3
1978-79	43	11.8	3.9	7.9
1979-80	⑤	9.3	6.1	3.2
1980-81	14	7.1	— 2.0	9.1
1981-82	21	— 2.6	— 7.4	4.8
1982-83	④	33.0	9.7	23.3
1983-84	13,	— 3.2	— 3.8	0.6
1984-85	32	19.0	12.1	6.9
1985-86	④	—22.5	3.9	—26.4
1986-87	22	9.3	12.5	— 3.2
1987-88	23	13.2	6.8	6.4
1988-89	14	30.0	6.4	23.6
1989-90	25	— 3.1	— 4.8	1.7
1990-91	18	18.8	12.6	6.2
Totals		**238.4%**	**86.0%**	**152.4%**
Average		**11.9%**	**4.3%**	**7.6%**

I began to follow this seasonal tendency in my investment newsletter, **Smart Money**, by reproducing the 112 NYSE common stocks hitting new lows in mid-December 1974. As you can see, the average rebound was 48.9% vs. the 22.1% gain for the NYSE composite. I have also seen these "unwanted children" outperforming the market in subsequent years—until the 1985-86 debacle when oil prices crumbled and three of the four new lows were oils.

Understandably, lower quality stocks tend to bounce back even higher than their bluer chip brethren. Santa Claus seems to reward pre-Christmas "scavengers" on Wall Street.

One small broker/money manager publicly claimed to achieve excellent results for his clients by establishing most of his positions during December, when stocks can be acquired at "wholesale" prices.

Examination of December purchases and sales by NYSE members through the years shows they tend to buy on balance during this month contrary to other months of the year. Perhaps they have known about the January Effect all these years (see page 104).

DECEMBER

MONDAY
7

Handwritten: 17.61   18.06 +.15   13,25+.08   28.88   +.12   44.28

Financial genius is a
rising stock market.
— John Kenneth Galbraith

TUESDAY
8

Handwritten: 17.70   18.13 +.07   13.27+.02   29.02 +.14   44.27 -.01

Become more humble as the
market goes your way.
— Bernard Baruch

WEDNESDAY
9

Handwritten: 17.77   18.09 -.04   13.24 -.03   28.88 -.14   44.09 -.18

I can calculate the motions of heavenly
bodies, but not the madness of people.
— Isaac Newton

THURSDAY
10

Handwritten: 17.92 -.17   13.22 -.02   43.8

When a lot of cash is waiting for a specific
decline on which to buy, the decline
usually refuses to materialize.
— Garfield A. Drew

FRIDAY
11

Handwritten: 17.83 -.09   13.19 -.03   28.72   43.68

One thing wrong with a self-made man,
he tends to worship his maker.
— Morris Raphael Cohen

SATURDAY
12

SUNDAY
13

THE SANTA CLAUS RALLY

Santa Claus comes to Wall Street nearly every year and brings a short, sweet, respectable rally. In the past 39 years, he failed to appear only in 1955, 1966, 1968, 1977, 1979, 1981, 1984 and 1990. The rally occurs within the last five days of the year (four prior to 1968) and the first two in January and is good for an average 1.72% gain.

DAILY % CHANGE IN S&P COMPOSITE INDEX AT YEAR END

	Trading Days Before Year-End							First Days in Jan.		
	7	6	5	4	3	2	1	1	2	3
1952	0.6	−0.4	0.1	0.2	0.6	0.7	−0.1	−0.1	0.5	−0.7
1953	−0.8	−0.3	0.4	−0.4	−0.6	0.9	0.2	0.6	0.6	0.2
1954	−0.1	0.1	−0.8	1.0	0.9	0.0	0.7	2.1	−0.9	0.3
1955	0.9	0.2	0.2	−0.6	−0.4	0.2	0.7	−0.7	−0.4	−0.1
1956	−0.2	−0.8	0.7	0.1	−0.1	0.4	0.2	−1.0	0.9	0.1
1957	−0.8	0.0	0.1	1.0	−0.4	−0.5	1.0	0.9	1.3	−0.5
1958	−0.1	−0.7	−0.5	1.3	1.2	0.3	0.5	0.4	0.4	−0.1
1959	−0.2	−0.3	0.1	−0.1	0.5	0.8	0.2	0.1	0.8	−0.4
1960	0.8	−0.3	0.1	0.1	0.5	0.5	0.1	−0.9	1.4	0.4
1961	−0.2	−0.4	0.1	0.2	0.9	0.1	−0.2	−0.8	0.2	−0.7
1962	0.4	−0.3	−0.1	0.6	−0.1	0.1	0.2	−0.7	1.6	0.7
1963	−0.2	−0.7	0.2	0.5	0.2	0.2	0.6	0.5	0.1	0.1
1964	−0.1	−0.2	0.0	−0.1	−0.3	0.6	0.5	0.6	0.5	0.3
1965	0.3	−0.1	−0.7	0.0	0.3	0.4	0.2	−0.3	0.1	0.7
1966	0.5	0.4	−0.3	−0.6	−0.5	−0.3	−0.1	0.1	0.2	1.3
1967	0.6	0.2	−0.2	0.1	0.7	0.0	0.6	−0.4	−0.5	−0.3
1968	−0.6	−0.1	−0.2	0.1	−0.4	−0.9	0.1	0.1	0.1	−1.5
1969	−0.9	−0.4	1.1	0.8	−0.7	0.4	0.5	1.0	0.5	−0.7
1970	0.1	0.1	0.6	0.5	1.1	0.2	−0.1	−1.1	0.7	0.6
1971	−0.6	−0.4	−0.2	1.0	0.3	−0.4	0.3	−0.4	0.4	1.0
1972	−0.5	−0.3	−0.6	0.6	0.3	0.5	1.0	0.9	0.4	−0.1
1973	−0.3	−1.1	−0.7	3.1	2.1	−0.2	0.0	0.1	2.2	−0.9
1974	−1.1	−1.4	1.4	0.8	−0.4	0.1	2.1	2.4	0.7	0.5
1975	−0.7	0.7	0.8	0.9	−0.1	−0.4	0.5	0.8	1.8	1.0
1976	0.5	0.1	1.2	0.7	−0.4	0.5	0.5	−0.4	−1.2	−0.9
1977	0.6	0.8	1.0	0.0	0.1	0.2	−0.2	−1.4	0.3	−0.8
1978	0.5	0.0	1.7	1.3	−0.9	−0.4	−0.2	0.6	1.1	0.8
1979	0.1	−0.6	0.1	0.1	0.2	−0.1	0.1	−2.0	−0.5	1.2
1980	1.6	−0.4	0.4	0.5	−1.1	0.2	0.3	0.4	1.2	0.1
1981	−0.4	−0.5	0.2	−0.2	−0.5	0.5	0.2	0.2	−2.2	−0.7
1982	0.2	0.6	1.8	−1.0	0.3	−0.6	0.2	−1.6	2.2	0.4
1983	1.0	−0.2	0.0	0.9	0.4	−0.3	0.0	−0.5	1.7	1.2
1984	−0.5	−0.5	0.8	0.2	−0.4	0.3	0.6	−1.1	−0.5	−0.5
1985	0.4	−1.1	−0.7	0.2	0.9	0.5	0.3	−0.8	0.6	−0.1
1986	−0.4	−1.0	0.2	0.1	−0.9	−0.5	−0.5	1.8	2.3	0.2
1987	0.2	1.3	−0.5	2.6	0.4	1.3	−0.3	3.6	0.3	0.9
1988	0.0	−0.2	0.4	−0.4	0.1	0.8	−0.6	−0.9	1.5	0.2
1989	0.1	0.6	0.8	−0.2	0.6	0.5	0.8	1.8	−0.3	−0.9
1990	−0.0	0.5	−0.6	0.3	−0.8	0.1	0.5	−1.1	−1.4	−0.3
Avg.	0.02	−0.18	0.39*	0.28	0.07	0.17	0.29	0.04	0.48	0.05

*From 1968 to date

Average 7-Day Gain: 1.72%

25 years had substantial gains of 0.9% to 7.1% during this holiday period. Of the other 14 years, seven had losses and seven had substandard gains of 0.4% to 0.7%. The bear markets of 1957, 1962, 1966, 1969, and 1977 were not preceded by Santa Claus rallies. Six other inferior periods preceded years when stocks could have been purchased at much lower prices later in the year (1956, 1965, 1968, 1978, 1980, and 1982). Just 1966, with tax selling down to the wire, proved to be the exception.

Getting back into the seasonal spirit: **If Santa Claus should fail to call, Bears may come to Broad & Wall.**

VGSTX   VTRSX   **DECEMBER**

17.71 -.12   13.18 +.01   28.67 -.05   **MONDAY**
                                                  # 14

Murphy & Slota — Analysis of deposits
                    and
                                                  Methodology is the last refuge
17.58 -.13   13.19 +.01   of a sterile mind.
                                                  — Marianne L. Simmel

                                28.63 -.04   **TUESDAY**
PPC Audits of Small Businesses — Course   # 15
Register — Holiday Inn - 18th & Market
        @ 8:45 A.M.   43.26

M
                                                  Don't put all your eggs in one basket.

17.62 +.04 | 13.18 -.01   28.57 -.06   **WEDNESDAY**
10:00 AM | — Murphy Slota   # 16

Murphy & Slota
Review estimated revenue + expense for year
Analysis of accounts   Brazil is the country of the future
Fossett costs   8 HRS ✓   and always will be.
                                                  — Brazilian joke

17.78 +.16   13.22 +.04   28.87 +.30   **THURSDAY**
Murphy & Slota   PSP   # 17
    Notice of amendment — amendment
    Notice of Pre-retirement Survivor
    Waiver of Annuity   2 Hrs ✓
                                                  Chance favors the prepared mind.
                                                  — Louis Pasteur

17.82 +.04   13.29 +.07   29.17 +.80   **FRIDAY**
                                                  ☠ ☠ ☠ # 18

                                                  Put your eggs in one basket
                                                  and watch the basket.

                                                  SATURDAY
                                                  # 19

                                                  SUNDAY
                                                  # 20

WINTER PORTFOLIO REVIEW

NO. OF SHARES	SECURITY	A ORIGINAL COST	B CURRENT VALUE	C GAIN (B-A) OR LOSS (A-B)	D % CHANGE (C÷A)	E MONTHS HELD	F CHANGE PER MO. (D÷E)	G ANNUAL RETURN (F×12)
200	Sample Corp.	$10,000	$10,400	$400	4.0%	8	0.5%	6.0%
TOTALS								

Stocks which have achieved their potential

1
2
3

Stocks which have been disappointments

1
2
3

Candidates for addition to portfolio

1
2
3

Investment decisions

1
2
3

DECEMBER

17.75 > .07   13.29 NC   29.10 - .07

MONDAY
21

You look at any giant corporation, and
I mean the biggies, and they all started
with a guy with an idea, doing it well.
— Irvine Robbins,
founded Baskin-Robbins

17.71 - .04   13.31 +.02   29.14 + .04

TUESDAY
22

Parkinson's Law: Work expands to fill
the time allotted to it.
— C. Northcote Parkinson

Sell VGTCX
17.91 +.28   13.30 -.01   28.13 -1.01

WEDNESDAY
23

When everyone is bearish, a market
must go up because there are no sellers
left; conversely, when everyone is
bullish, a market must go down
because there are no buyers left.

17.98 +.07   13.31 +.01   28.16 +.03

THURSDAY
24

Picture the entire United States run by
the U.S. Postal Service and you get
some idea of the bureaucratic mess
that prevails in the U.S.S.R.

Christmas
(Market Closed)

FRIDAY
25

In the stock market, the individual pits his
reason, his knowledge, his vision and his guts
against a variety of forces: his own human impulses;
the large and varied uncertainties of the future; and
the collective wisdom and irrationality of other investors.
— Charles J. Rolo

SATURDAY
26

SUNDAY
27

DIRECTORY OF SEASONAL TRADING PATTERNS

CONTENTS

18.07 +.09   1332 +.01   28.21 +.05

MONDAY

28

The man with a new idea is a crank —
until the idea succeeds.
— Mark Twain

18.08 +.01   12.88   28.28 +.07

TUESDAY

29

I don't know where speculators got a bad
name, since I know of no forward leap
which was not fathered by speculation.
— John Steinbeck

18.17 +.09   12.90 +.02   28.36 +.08

WEDNESDAY

30

Buy on the rumor, sell on the news.

THURSDAY

Sell VGTCX

31

Great spirits have always found violent
opposition from mediocrities.
— Albert Einstein

FRIDAY

**New Year's Day
(Market Closed)**

1

I know of no way of judging of the
future but by the past.
— Patrick Henry

SATURDAY

2

SUNDAY

3

A TYPICAL DAY IN THE MARKET

Market movements on a half-hourly basis are shown here since January 1987. Compared to the typical day during 1963 to 1985, the major difference now is stronger openings and closings in a more bullish market dominated by professionals. Morning and afternoon weakness appears one hour earlier.

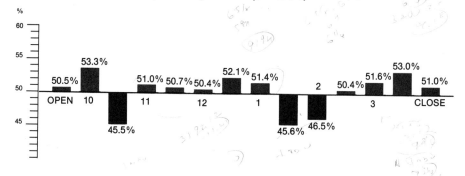

MARKET PERFORMANCE EACH HALF-HOUR OF THE DAY
(January 1987-April 1991)

Based on number of times Dow Jones Industrial average increased over previous half-hour

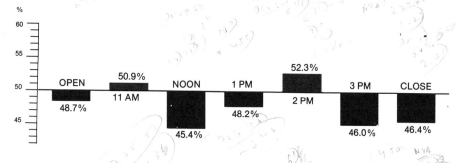

MARKET PERFORMANCE EACH HOUR OF THE DAY
(November 1963-June 1985)

Based on number of times Dow Jones Industrial average increased over previous hour

On the opposite page, half-hourly movements since January 1987 have been separated by day of the week. Visible proof of my discovery that Monday is the strongest comeback day of the week is evident. This is not surprising in as much as Monday is also the most massacred trading day. Other days tended to rise most often at the open. Fridays after lunch were two of the weakest half-hours of the week.

THROUGH THE WEEK ON A HALF-HOURLY BASIS

From the chart showing the percentage of times the Dow Jones industrial average rose over the preceding half-hour (January 1987 - April 1991 *) the typical week unfolds.

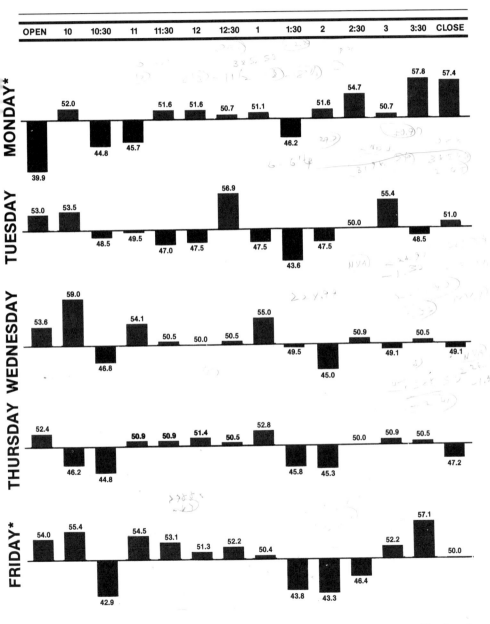

| OPEN | 10 | 10:30 | 11 | 11:30 | 12 | 12:30 | 1 | 1:30 | 2 | 2:30 | 3 | 3:30 | CLOSE |

*Research indicates that where Tuesday is the first trading day of the week, it follows the Monday pattern. Therefore, all such Tuesdays were combined with the Mondays here. Thursdays which are the final trading day of a given week behave like Fridays, and were similarly grouped with Fridays.

FRIDAYS RISE MORE TIMES THAN MONDAYS

A most unusual phenomenon in the stock market is the startling contrast between the first and last trading days of the week.

A tabulation of all the trading days in the 39-year period of June 1952—April 1991 reveals that the first trading day of the week (including Tuesday when Monday is a holiday) rises only 44.5% of the time. Conversely, the strongest day of the week is the last trading day of the week (including Thursday, when Friday is a holiday), when the market closes higher 57.8% of the time. Trading patterns could be changing as Thursdays were awful in 1990 and 1991.

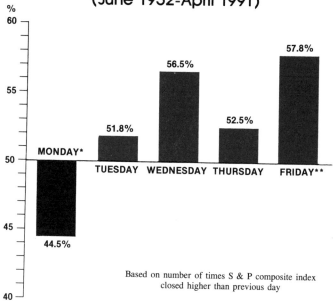

MARKET PERFORMANCE EACH DAY OF THE WEEK
(June 1952-April 1991)

Based on number of times S & P composite index closed higher than previous day

*On Monday holidays, the following Tuesday is included in the Monday figure.
**On Friday holidays, the preceding Thursday is included in the Friday figure.

THE DOWN-ON-FRIDAY/DOWN-ON-MONDAY EFFECT

In the 1970 Almanac I reported on the profound effect of Friday's activity on Monday's markets. As discovered by Frank Cross of Niederhoffer, Cross & Zeckhauser—when the market is down on Friday, chances are three to one that Monday will also decline. In the 1953-1985 period, I found that only 28.2% of the Mondays were able to rise after declining Fridays. A cluster of three or four up–Mondays following down–Fridays occurred around important market bottoms in 1966, 1968, 1970, 1973, 1974 and 1982, which is highly significant. Six of seven down–Fridays in the fall of 1986 followed by up- Mondays presaged the eruption of 1987. Half of the down–Fridays since 1988 were followed by up–Mondays.

DAILY PERFORMANCE EACH YEAR SINCE 1952

To determine if market trend alters performance of different days of the week, I separated the thirteen bear years of 1953, 57, 60, 62, 66, 69, 70, 73, 74, 77, 81, 84, and 90 from the 26 bull market years. While middle days—Tuesday, Wednesday and Thursday—did not vary much on average between bull and bear years, Mondays and Fridays were sharply affected by changes in market climate. There was a swing of 10.5 percentage points in Monday's performance and 11.5 percentage points in Friday's.

PERCENTAGE OF TIMES MARKET
CLOSED HIGHER THAN PREVIOUS DAY
(Based on S&P composite index, 1952-1991)

Year	Monday	Tuesday	Wednesday	Thursday	Friday
1952	50.0%	57.7%	56.7%	61.5%	65.5%
1953	32.7	47.9	54.9	60.8	56.6
1954	51.9	57.4	63.5	60.0	73.1
1955	48.1	45.7	67.3	60.8	80.8
1956	34.0	40.0	44.9	50.0	61.5
1957	25.0	58.0	64.7	46.8	46.2
1958	59.6	53.1	59.6	68.1	73.1
1959	40.4	51.0	58.3	51.0	69.2
1960	36.5	52.2	44.2	56.3	61.5
1961	53.8	54.3	62.0	54.0	64.2
1962	28.3	52.1	58.0	51.0	50.0
1963	46.2	63.3	51.0	57.4	69.2
1964	40.4	48.0	62.7	59.6	78.8
1965	46.2	52.1	55.8	51.0	69.2
1966	36.5	47.8	53.8	42.0	57.7
1967	40.4	52.2	58.8	64.0	63.5
1968*	39.1	65.0	60.9	45.0	56.5
1969	32.1	46.9	50.0	67.4	52.8
1970	38.5	44.0	63.5	46.8	51.9
1971	44.2	62.5	55.8	50.0	55.8
1972	38.5	60.4	55.8	51.0	67.3
1973	30.8	51.1	52.9	44.9	42.3
1974	34.6	56.3	52.0	38.8	34.6
1975	53.8	38.8	59.6	58.3	57.7
1976	55.8	56.5	55.8	40.8	56.6
1977	40.4	40.4	46.2	53.1	55.8
1978	51.9	43.5	59.6	54.0	48.1
1979	54.7	51.0	58.8	66.0	44.2
1980	57.6	56.2	69.8	33.3	59.6
1981	46.2	38.8	53.8	54.2	46.2
1982	44.2	39.6	44.2	46.0	48.1
1983	50.0	46.8	59.6	52.0	55.8
1984	39.6	62.5	30.8	44.9	44.2
1985	44.2	59.2	52.9	57.1	52.9
1986	50.0	44.9	67.3	56.3	55.8
1987	50.0	59.2	63.5	54.0	46.2
1988	51.9	63.8	51.9	44.0	59.6
1989	51.9	47.8	69.2	58.0	69.2
1990	66.7	52.2	52.0	38.8	51.1
1991**	44.4	50.0	61.1	41.2	61.1
Average	**44.5%**	**51.8%**	**56.5%**	**52.5%**	**57.8%**
26 Bull Years	**48.0%**	**52.7%**	**58.7%**	**54.0%**	**61.6%**
13 Bear Years	**37.5%**	**50.0%**	**52.1%**	**49.7%**	**50.1%**

*Excludes last six months of four-day market weeks.
**Four months only. Not included in averages.

THE MONTHLY FIVE-DAY BULGE

The market rises more often (60.7%) on the second trading day of the month and a period of five consecutive trading days, the last, first, second, third, and fourth, distinctly outperforms the rest of the days of the month. In a 468-month study (May 1952-April 1991) the market was up 57.6% of the time on these five bullish days, as compared to an average of 50.8% for the remaining sixteen trading days of a typical month.

This occurs because individuals and institutions tend to operate on a monthly fiscal basis. Big cash inflows at banks, funds and insurance companies occur around the end or beginnning of the month and often cause upward pressure. (See pages 54 and 56.)

Much of the market strength in these 39 years has centered around the last plus the first four trading days of the month. While the market has risen on average 52.4% of the time, the **prime five days** have risen 57.6%.

Sophisticated short-term traders, floor specialists, and portfolio managers could benefit immensely by studying this month-end/beginning upward bias. It would be difficult for long-term investors to take advantage of this phenomenon.

I have observed the market many times at month's end pausing during a sharp downturn, spurting after a resting or quiet phase, or accelerating its previously gradual rate of climb during a bull market.

Over 25 years of monthly best-five-days results are listed on page 56. Index future expirations seemed to have thrown the strategy off in 1985 and 1986 until expiration times were adjusted. Also February and July have tended to be losers since 1973.

Several portfolios have been managed successfully for over a dozen years by switching back and forth between no-load growth funds for each month's prime five days and to a money market fund for the rest of the month's trading days.

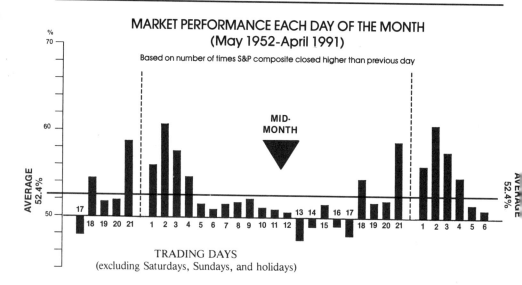

MARKET PERFORMANCE EACH DAY OF THE MONTH
(May 1952-April 1991)

Based on number of times S&P composite closed higher than previous day

TRADING DAYS
(excluding Saturdays, Sundays, and holidays)

NOVEMBER, DECEMBER, AND JANUARY
YEAR'S BEST THREE-MONTH SPAN

The most important observation to be made from a chart showing the average monthly % change in market prices since 1950 is that institutions (mutual funds, pension funds, banks, etc.) determine the trading patterns in today's market.

MARKET PERFORMANCE EACH MONTH OF THE YEAR
40⅓ Years (January 1950-April 1991)

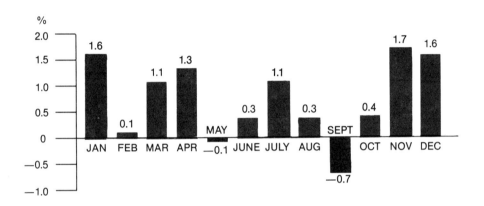

Average month-to-month % change in Standard & Poor's composite index
(Based on monthly closing prices)

The "investment calendar" reflects the annual, semi-annual and quarterly operations of institutions during January, April and July. October, besides being a "tight money" month, the beginning of the new car year, and the last campaign month before elections, is also the time when most bear markets seem to end, as in 1946, 1957, 1960, 1966, 1974, 1987, and 1990. (August was most favored in 1982, 1984, 1986 and 1987.)

Unusual year-end strength comes from corporate and private pension funds producing a 4.8% gain average between October 31 and January 31.

Between 1934 and 1949, when the market stayed within the one-hundred to two-hundred range in the Dow Jones industrial average, January, June, July, and October stood out as the strongest months of the year. It is obvious that a decided shift in investment seasons has occurred in recent years.

The most volatile months in both directions have been January, far out front, followed by August, November and July. December has been the least dangerous month. April and March are also relatively safe.

See page 38 for monthly performance tables for the S&P 500 and the Dow Jones industrials. See page 40 for unique six-month switching strategy.

2OTH CENTURY BULL AND BEAR MARKETS

— Beginning —		— Ending —		Bull		Bear	
Date	DJIA	Date	DJIA	% Gain	Days	% Change	Days
09/24/00	52.96	06/17/01	78.26	47.8	266	−46.1	875
11/09/03	42.15	01/19/06	103.00	144.4	802	−48.5	665
11/15/07	53.00	11/19/09	100.53	89.7	735	−27.4	675
09/25/11	72.94	09/30/12	94.15	29.1	371	−24.1	668
12/24/14	53.17	11/21/16	110.15	107.2	698	−40.1	393
12/19/17	65.95	11/03/19	119.62	81.4	684	−46.6	660
08/24/21	63.90	03/20/23	105.38	64.9	573	−18.6	221
10/27/23	85.76	09/03/29	381.17	344.5	2138	−47.9	71
11/13/29	198.69	04/17/30	294.07	48.0	155	−86.0	813
07/08/32	41.22	09/07/32	79.93	93.9	61	−37.2	173
02/27/33	50.16	02/05/34	110.74	120.8	343	−22.8	171
07/26/34	85.51	03/10/37	194.40	127.3	958	−49.1	386
03/31/38	98.95	11/12/38	158.41	60.1	226	−23.3	147
04/08/39	121.44	09/12/39	155.92	28.4	157	−40.4	959
04/28/42	92.92	05/29/46	212.50	128.7	1492	−23.2	353
05/17/47	163.21	06/15/48	193.16	18.4	395	−16.3	363
06/13/49	161.60	01/05/53	293.79	81.8	1302	−13.0	252
09/14/53	255.49	04/06/56	521.05	103.9	935	−19.4	564
10/22/57	419.79	01/05/60	685.47	63.3	805	−17.4	294
10/25/60	566.05	12/13/61	734.91	29.8	414	−27.1	195
06/26/62	535.76	02/09/66	995.15	85.7	1324	−25.2	240
10/07/66	744.32	12/03/68	985.21	32.4	788	−35.9	539
05/26/70	631.16	04/28/71	950.82	50.6	337	−16.1	209
11/23/71	797.97	01/11/73	1051.70	31.8	415	−45.1	694
12/06/74	577.60	09/21/76	1014.79	75.7	655	−26.9	525
02/28/78	742.12	09/08/78	907.74	22.3	192	−16.4	591
04/21/80	759.13	04/27/81	1024.05	34.9	371	−24.1	472
08/12/82	776.92	11/29/83	1287.20	65.7	474	−15.6	238
07/24/84	1086.57	08/25/87	2722.42	150.6	1127	−36.1	55
10/19/87	1738.74	07/17/90	2999.75	72.5	972	−21.2	86
10/11/90	2365.10						

Data: Ned Davis Research

Bear markets begin at the end of one bull market and end at the start of the next bull market (7/17/90 to 10/11/90 as an example).

WINNING STRATEGIES IN SECONDS

In the stock market, the individual pits his reason, his knowledge, his vision and his guts against a variety of forces; his own human impulses; the large and varied uncertainties of the future; and the collective wisdom and irrationality of other investors.   —Charles J. Rolo

Quite true! But arm that individual with the revolutionary software that I have been using and suddenly he, or she, stands twenty feet taller than other investors. And, more important, the system operates WITHOUT A PROGRAMMER!

The Market Information Machine (MIM) includes a Sun Workstation and is the fastest brain on Wall Street. The software uses simple English and in a flash can determine the feasibility of any system or strategy you can devise. You can correlate hundreds of economic or technical indicators with the Dow, S&P, individual stocks, industry groups, mutual funds or commodity futures. Consider the possibilities that the Market Information Machine can provide:

- You can see charts of the Dow on the five days during and after all 37 triple-witching weeks since 1982 showing how many Dow points were gained or lost in each of those weeks.

- See the best time of the year to buy or sell toy stocks, oil refiners, airlines, soybeans, sugar, wheat, corn, Swiss Francs, orange juice, platinum or pork bellies.

- See any stock five days before and after dividends; at the beginning or end of a month; when quarterly earnings are announced; with moving averages or relative strength.

- Know the best stocks to buy or sell when interest rates, the CPI, gold or unemployment rises or falls.

- Discern which industries top out first or turn up first in market cycles. Which industries or stocks are laggards.

- Discover which combination of indicators gives the best sell signal in a bull market—the best buy signal in a bear market.

- Find which moving average gives the best buy and sell signals for each listed stock.

- Figure which combination of "best days of the week," "best days of the month" and "best months of the year" produce the best investment results.

I have been using The Market Information Machine for the past year and I am still amazed at its endless possibilities. All the data in the 25th Edition of this Almanac can now be obtained in an instant instead of hours or days.

If you have an unusual idea about any new indicator, market trend or strategy, just give us a call and we'll put the Market Information Machine to work.

DECENNIAL CYCLE: A MARKET PHENOMENON

By arranging each year's market gain or loss so that all the first years of each decade fall into the same column, etc., certain interesting patterns emerge—strong fifth and eighth years, weak seventh and zero years, etc.

This fascinating phenomenon was presented by Edgar Lawrence Smith in *Common Stocks and Business Cycles* (William-Frederick Press, 4th rev. ed., 1970).

When Smith first cut graphs of market prices into ten-year segments and placed them above one another, he observed that each decade tended to have three bull market cycles. It might also be pointed out that the longest and strongest bull markets seem to favor the middle years of a decade. Anthony Gaubis co-pioneered the decennial pattern with Smith.

Since the 1920s, low points of decades have been reached much earlier than in the previous fifty years.

The next major bear market in this decennial cycle will likely occur in 1993 or 1994.

THE TEN-YEAR STOCK MARKET CYCLE

Annual % change in Standard & Poor's Composite Index Past 100 Years

DECADES	Year of Decade									
	1st	2nd	3rd	4th	5th	6th	7th	8th	9th	10th
1881-1890	—	—	—	—	20	9	— 7	— 2	3	—14
1891-1900	18	1	—20	— 3	1	— 2	13	19	7	14
1901-1910	16	1	—19	25	16	3	—33	37	14	—12
1911-1920	1	3	—14	— 9	32	3	—31	16	13	—24
1921-1930	7	20	— 3	19	23	5	26	36	—15	—29
1931-1940	—47	—18	48	— 2	39	28	—34	13	0	—12
1941-1950	—15	6	21	14	33	—10	— 2	— 2	11	20
1951-1960	15	7	— 3	39	23	4	—13	33	11	— 4
1961-1970	27	—13	18	13	9	—11	17	12	—14	— 1
1971-1980	10	12	—19	—32	32	18	—10	2	11	26
1981-1990	— 7	13	18	0	26	20	— 3	15	26	—6
1991-2000										
Up Years	7	8	4	6	11	8	3	9	9	3
Down Years	3	2	6	4	0	3	8	2	2	8
Total % Change	25%	32%	27%	64%	254%	67%	—77%	179%	67%	—42%

Based on average December prices.

PRESIDENTIAL ELECTION/STOCK MARKET CYCLE
THE 159-YEAR SAGA CONTINUES

Each president of the United States must face political realities every four years if he wants to stay in the White House, or at least keep his party in power. It is no mere coincidence that the last two years (election year and pre-election year) of the 41 administrations since 1832 produced a total net market gain of 527%, dwarfing the 74% gain of the first two years of these administrations.

In a reversal of form, election-year 1984 was flat and post-election 1985 and mid-term 1986 were sharply higher. The strong secular bull market pushed the Dow up another 800 points by mid-1987 but the biggest crash in history made this pre-election year the worst in 40 years. Watch out for 1993!

STOCK MARKET ACTION SINCE 1832
Net change from year to year based on average December prices

PRESIDENT ELECTED	4-year cycle beginning	Election Year	Post-Election Year	Mid-term	Pre-Election Year
Jackson (D)	1832	15%	— 3%	10%	2%
Van Buren (D)	1836	— 8	— 8	1	—13
W.H. Harrison (W)**	1840*	5	—14	—13	36
Polk (D)	1844*	8	6	—15	1
Taylor (W)**	1848*	— 4	0	19	— 3
Pierce (D)	1852*	20	—13	—30	1
Buchanan (D)	1856	4	—30	— 7	— 7
Lincoln (R)	1860*	— 4	— 4	43	30
Lincoln (R)**	1864	0	—14	— 3	— 6
Grant (R)	1868	2	— 7	— 4	7
Grant (R)	1872	7	—13	3	— 4
Hayes (R)	1876	—18	—10	6	43
Garfield (R)**	1880	19	3	— 3	— 9
Cleveland (D)	1884*	—19	20	9	— 7
B. Harrison (R)	1888*	— 2	3	—14	18
Cleveland (D)	1892*	1	—20	— 3	1
McKinley (R)	1896*	— 2	13	19	7
McKinley (R)**	1900	14	16	1	—19
T. Roosevelt (R)	1904	25	16	3	—33
Taft (R)	1908	37	14	—12	1
Wilson (D)	1912*	3	—14	— 9	32
Wilson (D)	1916	3	—31	16	13
Harding (R)**	1920*	—24	7	20	— 3
Coolidge (R)	1924	19	23	5	26
Hoover (R)	1928	36	—15	—29	—47
F. Roosevelt (D)	1932*	—18	48	— 2	39
F. Roosevelt (D)	1936	28	—34	13	0
F. Roosevelt (D)	1940	—12	—15	6	21
F. Roosevelt (D)**	1944	14	33	—10	— 2
Truman (D)	1948	— 2	11	20	15
Eisenhower (R)	1952*	7	— 3	39	23
Eisenhower (R)	1956	4	—13	33	11
Kennedy (D)**	1960*	— 4	27	—13	18
Johnson (D)	1964	13	9	—11	17
Nixon (R)	1968*	12	—14	— 1	10
Nixon (R)***	1972	12	—19	—32	32
Carter (D)	1976*	18	—10	2	11
Reagan (R)	1980*	26	— 7	13	18
Reagan (R)	1984	0	26	20	— 3
Bush (R)	1988	15	26	— 6	
1904—1991 totals		212%	65%	65%	199%
1832—1991 totals		250%	—10%	84%	277%

*Party in power ousted **Death in office ***Resigned **D**—Democrat, **W**—Whig, **R**—Republican 125

MONTHLY PERCENT CHANGES IN STANDARD & POOR'S 500

Year	JAN	FEB	MAR	APR	MAY	JUNE	JUL	AUG	SEP	OCT	NOV	DEC	Year's Change
1950	1.7%	1.0%	0.4%	4.5%	3.9%	-5.8%	0.8%	3.3%	5.6%	0.4%	-0.1%	4.6%	21.8%
1951	6.1	0.6	-1.8	4.8	-4.1	-2.6	6.9	3.9	-0.1	-1.4	-0.3	3.9	16.5
1952	1.6	-3.6	4.8	-4.3	2.3	4.6	1.8	-1.5	-2.0	-0.1	4.6	3.5	11.8
1953	-0.7	-1.8	-2.4	-2.6	-0.3	-1.6	2.5	-5.8	0.1	5.1	0.9	0.2	-6.6
1954	5.1	0.3	3.1	4.5	3.7	0.1	5.7	-3.4	8.3	-1.9	8.1	5.1	45.0
1955	1.8	0.4	-0.5	3.8	-0.1	8.2	6.1	-0.8	1.1	-3.0	7.5	-0.1	26.4
1956	-3.6	3.5	6.9	-0.2	-6.6	3.9	5.2	-3.8	-4.5	0.5	-1.1	3.5	2.6
1957	-4.2	-3.3	2.0	3.7	3.7	-0.1	1.1	-5.6	-6.2	-3.2	1.6	-4.1	-14.3
1958	4.3	-2.1	3.1	3.2	1.5	2.6	4.3	1.2	4.8	2.5	2.2	5.2	38.1
1959	0.4	0.0	0.1	3.9	1.9	-0.4	3.5	-1.5	-4.6	1.1	1.3	2.8	8.5
1960	-7.1	0.9	-1.4	-1.8	2.7	2.0	-2.5	2.6	-6.0	-0.2	4.0	4.6	-3.0
1961	6.3	2.7	2.6	0.4	1.9	-2.9	3.3	2.0	-2.0	2.8	3.9	0.3	23.1
1962	-3.8	1.6	-0.6	-6.2	-8.6	-8.2	6.4	1.5	-4.8	0.4	10.2	1.3	-11.8
1963	4.9	-2.9	3.5	4.9	1.4	-2.0	-0.3	4.9	-1.1	3.2	-1.1	2.5	18.9
1964	2.7	1.0	1.5	0.6	1.1	1.6	1.8	-1.6	2.9	0.8	-0.5	0.4	13.0
1965	3.3	-0.1	-1.5	3.4	-0.8	-4.9	1.3	2.3	3.2	2.7	-0.9	0.9	9.1
1966	0.5	-1.8	-2.2	2.1	-5.4	-1.6	-1.3	-7.8	-0.7	4.8	0.3	-0.1	-13.1
1967	7.8	0.2	3.9	4.2	-5.2	1.8	4.5	-1.2	3.3	-2.9	0.1	2.6	20.1
1968	-4.4	-3.1	0.9	8.2	1.1	0.9	-1.8	1.1	3.9	0.7	4.8	-4.2	7.7
1969	-0.8	-4.7	3.4	2.1	-0.2	-5.6	-6.0	4.0	-2.5	4.4	-3.5	-1.9	-11.4
1970	-7.6	5.3	0.1	-9.0	-6.1	-5.0	7.3	4.4	3.3	-1.1	4.7	5.7	0.1
1971	4.0	0.9	3.7	3.6	-4.2	0.1	-4.1	3.6	-0.7	-4.2	-0.3	8.6	10.8
1972	1.8	2.5	0.6	0.4	1.7	-2.2	0.2	3.4	-0.5	0.9	4.6	1.2	15.6
1973	-1.7	-3.7	-0.1	-4.1	-1.9	-0.7	3.8	-3.7	4.0	-0.1	-11.4	1.7	-17.4
1974	-1.0	-0.4	-2.3	-3.9	-3.4	-1.5	-7.8	-9.0	-11.9	16.3	-5.3	-2.0	-29.7
1975	12.3	6.0	2.2	4.7	4.4	4.4	-6.8	-2.1	-3.5	6.2	2.5	-1.2	31.5
1976	11.8	-1.1	3.1	-1.1	-1.4	4.1	-0.8	-0.5	2.3	-2.2	-0.8	5.2	19.1
1977	-5.1	-2.2	-1.4	0.02	-2.4	4.5	-1.6	-2.1	-0.7	-4.3	2.7	0.3	-11.5
1978	-6.2	-2.5	2.5	8.5	0.5	-1.8	5.4	2.6	-0.7	-9.2	1.7	1.5	1.1
1979	4.0	-3.7	5.5	0.2	-2.6	3.9	0.9	5.3	0.0	-6.9	4.3	1.7	12.3
1980	5.8	-0.4	-10.2	4.1	4.7	2.7	6.5	0.6	2.5	1.6	10.2	-3.4	25.8
1981	-4.6	1.3	3.6	-2.3	-0.2	-1.0	-0.2	-6.2	-5.4	4.9	3.7	-3.0	-9.7
1982	-1.8	-6.1	-1.0	4.0	-3.9	-2.0	-2.3	11.6	0.8	11.0	3.6	1.5	14.8
1983	3.3	1.9	3.3	7.5	-1.2	3.5	-3.3	1.1	1.0	-1.5	1.7	-0.9	17.3
1984	-0.9	-3.9	1.3	0.5	-5.9	1.7	-1.6	10.6	-0.3	-0.01	-1.5	2.2	1.4
1985	7.3	0.9	-0.3	-0.5	5.4	1.2	-0.5	-1.2	-3.5	4.3	6.5	4.5	26.3
1986	0.2	7.1	5.3	-1.4	5.0	1.4	-5.9	7.1	-8.5	5.5	2.1	-2.8	14.6
1987	13.2	3.7	2.6	-1.1	0.6	4.8	4.8	3.5	-2.4	-21.8	-8.5	7.3	2.0
1988	4.0	4.2	-3.3	0.9	0.3	4.3	-0.5	-3.9	4.0	2.6	-1.9	1.5	12.4
1989	7.1	-2.9	2.1	5.0	3.5	-0.8	8.8	1.6	-0.7	2.5	1.7	2.1	27.3
1990	-6.9	0.9	2.4	-2.7	9.2	-0.9	-0.5	-9.4	-5.1	-0.7	6.0	2.5	-6.6
1991	4.2	6.7	2.2	0.03	3.9	-4.8	4.5	2.0	-1.9	1.2	-4.4	11.2	26.3

MONTHLY CLOSING PRICES IN STANDARD & POOR'S 500

Year	DEC	NOV	OCT	SEP	AUG	JUL	JUNE	MAY	APR	MAR	FEB	JAN	Year
1950	20.41	19.51	19.53	19.45	18.42	17.84	17.69	18.78	18.07	17.29	17.22	17.05	1950
1951	23.77	22.88	22.94	23.26	23.28	22.40	20.96	21.52	22.43	21.40	21.80	21.66	1951
1952	26.57	25.66	24.52	24.54	25.03	25.40	24.96	23.86	23.32	24.37	23.26	24.14	1952
1953	24.81	24.76	24.54	23.35	23.32	24.75	24.14	24.54	24.62	25.29	25.90	26.38	1953
1954	35.98	34.24	31.68	32.31	29.83	30.88	29.21	29.19	28.16	26.96	26.15	26.08	1954
1955	45.48	45.51	42.34	43.67	43.18	43.52	41.03	37.91	37.96	36.58	36.76	36.63	1955
1956	46.67	45.08	45.58	45.35	47.51	49.39	46.97	45.20	48.38	48.48	45.34	43.82	1956
1957	39.99	41.72	41.06	42.42	45.22	47.91	47.37	47.43	45.74	44.11	43.26	44.72	1957
1958	55.21	52.48	51.33	50.06	47.75	47.19	45.24	44.09	43.44	42.10	40.84	41.70	1958
1959	59.89	58.28	57.52	56.88	59.60	60.51	58.47	58.68	57.59	55.44	55.41	55.42	1959
1960	58.11	55.54	53.39	53.52	56.96	55.51	56.92	55.83	54.37	55.34	56.12	55.61	1960
1961	71.56	71.32	68.62	66.73	68.07	66.76	64.64	66.56	65.31	65.06	63.44	61.78	1961
1962	63.10	62.26	56.52	56.27	59.12	58.23	54.75	59.63	65.24	69.55	69.96	68.84	1962
1963	75.02	73.20	74.01	71.70	72.50	69.13	69.37	70.80	69.80	66.57	64.29	66.20	1963
1964	84.75	84.42	84.86	84.18	81.83	83.18	81.69	80.37	79.46	78.98	77.80	77.04	1964
1965	92.43	91.61	92.42	89.96	87.17	85.25	84.12	88.42	89.11	86.16	87.43	87.56	1965
1966	80.33	80.45	80.20	76.56	77.10	83.60	84.74	86.13	91.06	89.23	91.22	92.88	1966
1967	96.47	94.00	93.90	96.71	93.64	94.75	90.64	89.08	94.01	90.20	86.78	86.61	1967
1968	103.86	108.37	103.41	102.67	98.86	97.74	99.58	98.68	97.59	90.20	89.36	92.24	1968
1969	92.06	93.81	97.24	93.12	95.51	91.83	97.71	103.46	103.69	101.51	98.13	103.01	1969
1970	92.15	87.20	83.25	84.21	81.52	78.05	72.72	76.55	81.52	89.63	89.50	85.02	1970
1971	102.09	93.99	94.23	98.34	99.03	95.58	99.70	99.63	103.95	100.31	96.75	95.88	1971
1972	118.05	116.67	111.58	110.55	111.09	107.39	107.14	109.53	107.67	107.20	106.57	103.94	1972
1973	97.55	95.96	108.29	108.43	104.25	108.22	104.26	104.95	106.97	111.52	111.68	116.03	1973
1974	68.56	69.97	73.90	63.54	72.15	79.31	86.00	87.28	90.31	93.98	96.22	96.57	1974
1975	90.19	91.24	89.04	83.87	86.88	88.75	95.19	91.15	87.30	83.36	81.59	76.98	1975
1976	107.46	102.10	102.90	105.24	102.91	103.44	104.28	100.18	101.64	102.77	99.82	100.86	1976
1977	95.10	94.83	92.34	96.53	96.77	98.85	100.48	96.12	98.44	98.42	99.71	102.03	1977
1978	96.11	94.70	93.15	102.54	103.29	100.68	95.53	97.29	96.83	89.21	87.04	89.25	1978
1979	107.94	106.16	101.82	109.32	109.32	103.81	102.91	99.08	101.76	101.59	96.28	99.93	1979
1980	135.76	140.52	127.47	125.46	122.38	121.67	114.24	111.24	106.29	102.09	113.66	114.16	1980
1981	122.55	126.35	121.89	116.18	122.79	130.92	131.21	132.59	132.87	136.00	131.27	129.55	1981
1982	140.64	138.54	133.71	120.45	119.51	107.09	109.61	111.88	116.44	111.96	113.11	120.40	1982
1983	164.93	166.40	163.55	166.07	164.40	162.56	168.11	162.39	164.42	152.96	148.06	145.30	1983
1984	167.24	163.58	166.09	166.10	166.68	150.66	153.18	150.55	160.05	159.18	157.06	163.41	1984
1985	211.28	202.17	189.32	182.08	188.63	190.92	191.85	189.55	179.83	180.66	181.18	179.63	1985
1986	242.17	249.22	243.98	231.32	252.93	236.12	250.84	247.35	235.52	238.90	226.92	211.78	1986
1987	247.08	230.30	251.79	321.83	329.80	318.66	304.00	290.10	288.36	291.70	284.20	274.08	1987
1988	277.72	273.70	278.97	271.91	261.52	272.02	273.50	262.16	261.33	258.89	267.82	257.07	1988
1989	353.40	345.99	340.36	349.15	351.45	346.09	317.98	320.52	309.64	294.87	288.86	297.47	1989
1990	330.22	322.22	304.00	306.05	322.56	356.15	358.02	361.23	330.80	339.94	331.89	329.08	1990
1991									375.35	375.22	367.07	343.93	1991

MONTHLY POINT CHANGES IN DOW JONES INDUSTRIALS

Year	JAN	FEB	MAR	APR	MAY	JUNE	JUL	AUG	SEP	OCT	NOV	DEC	Year's Close
1950	1.66	1.65	2.61	8.28	9.09	-14.31	0.29	7.47	9.49	1.35	2.59	7.81	235.41
1951	13.42	3.22	4.11	11.19	9.48	-7.01	15.22	12.39	0.91	-8.81	1.08	7.96	269.23
1952	1.46	-10.61	9.38	-11.83	5.31	11.32	5.30	4.52	-4.43	-1.38	14.43	8.24	291.90
1953	-2.13	5.50	-4.40	-5.12	2.47	-4.02	7.12	-14.16	-2.82	11.77	5.56	0.47	280.90
1954	11.49	2.15	8.97	15.82	8.16	6.04	14.39	-12.12	24.66	-8.32	34.63	17.62	404.39
1955	4.44	3.04	2.17	15.95	0.79	26.52	14.47	2.33	1.56	-11.75	28.39	5.14	488.40
1956	-17.66	12.91	28.14	4.33	-38.07	14.73	25.03	-15.77	-26.79	4.60	7.07	26.69	499.47
1957	20.31	-14.54	10.19	19.55	10.57	1.64	5.23	-24.17	-28.05	-15.26	8.83	-14.18	435.69
1958	14.33	-10.10	6.84	9.10	6.84	15.48	24.81	5.64	23.46	11.13	14.24	26.19	583.65
1959	10.31	9.54	1.79	22.04	20.04	0.19	31.28	10.47	-32.73	14.92	12.58	20.18	679.36
1960	56.74	7.50	-13.53	-14.89	23.80	15.12	-23.89	9.26	-45.85	0.22	16.86	18.67	615.89
1961	32.31	13.88	14.55	2.08	18.01	-12.76	21.41	14.57	-18.73	2.71	17.68	9.54	731.14
1962	-31.14	8.05	1.10	-41.62	-51.97	-52.08	36.65	11.25	-30.20	10.79	59.53	2.80	652.10
1963	30.75	-19.91	19.58	35.18	9.26	-20.08	-11.45	33.89	3.47	22.44	4.71	12.43	762.95
1964	22.39	14.80	13.15	-2.52	9.79	10.94	9.60	2.62	36.89	2.29	2.35	-1.30	874.12
1965	28.73	0.62	-14.43	8.91	-4.27	-50.01	13.71	11.36	37.48	30.24	14.11	22.55	969.26
1966	14.25	-31.62	-27.12	31.07	-49.61	-13.97	-22.72	2.95	25.37	32.85	3.93	5.90	785.69
1967	64.20	-10.52	26.61	71.55	-44.49	7.70	43.98	13.01	39.78	46.92	32.69	29.60	905.11
1968	49.64	-14.97	0.17	14.70	-13.22	-1.20	-14.80	21.25	23.63	16.60	43.69	-41.33	943.75
1969	-2.30	-40.84	30.27	-49.50	-12.62	-64.37	-57.72	30.46	3.90	42.90	38.48	-11.94	800.36
1970	56.30	33.53	7.98	37.38	-35.63	-16.91	50.59	39.64	10.88	5.07	7.66	44.83	838.92
1971	29.58	10.33	25.54		-33.94	-16.67	-32.71	38.99	10.46	48.19	62.69	58.86	890.20
1972	11.97	25.96	12.57	13.47	6.55	-31.69	-4.29	38.83	59.53	2.25		1.81	1020.02
1973	21.00	-43.95	-4.06	-29.58	-20.02	9.70	34.69	78.85	70.71	9.48	-134.33	28.61	850.86
1974	4.69	4.98	-13.85	-9.93	-34.58	0.24	-44.98	3.83	-41.46	57.65	46.86	2.42	616.24
1975	87.45	35.36	29.10	53.19	10.95	46.70	-47.48	10.90	16.45	42.16	24.63	-8.26	852.41
1976	122.87	-2.67	26.84	-2.60	-21.62	27.55	-26.23	28.58	14.38	25.26	17.71	57.43	1004.65
1977	50.28	-17.95	-17.29	7.77	-28.24	17.64	-18.14	14.55	11.00	28.76	11.35	1.47	831.17
1978	61.25	-27.80	15.24	79.96	3.29	-21.66	43.32	41.21	9.05	73.37	6.58	5.98	805.01
1979	34.21	-30.40	53.36	-7.28	-32.57	19.65	4.44	2.73	0.17	62.88	6.65	16.39	838.74
1980	37.11	-12.71	-77.39	31.31	33.79	17.07	67.40	70.87	31.49	7.93	68.85	-29.35	963.99
1981	-16.72	27.31	29.29	-6.12	-6.00	-14.87	-24.54	92.71	5.06	2.57	36.43	-13.98	875.00
1982	3.90	-46.71	-1.62	25.59	-28.82	-7.61	-3.33	16.94	16.97	95.47	47.56	7.26	1046.54
1983	29.16	36.92	17.41	96.17	-26.22	21.98	-22.74	109.10	-17.67	7.93	50.82	-17.38	1258.64
1984	38.06	-65.95	10.26	5.86	-65.90	27.55	-17.12	13.44	5.38	0.67	18.44	22.63	1211.57
1985	75.20	-2.76	-17.23	8.72	57.35	20.05	11.99	123.03		45.68	97.82	74.54	1546.67
1986	24.32	138.07	109.55	-34.63	92.73	16.01	-117.41	90.88	-130.76	110.23	36.42	-18.28	1895.95
1987	262.09	65.95	80.70	-18.33	5.21	126.96	153.54	97.08	66.67	-602.75	-159.98	105.28	1938.83
1988	19.39	113.40	-83.56	44.27	-1.21	110.59	-12.98	81.26	81.26	35.74	34.14	54.06	2168.57
1989	173.75	-83.93	35.23	125.18	61.35	-40.09	220.60	76.61	44.45	-47.74	61.19	46.93	2753.20
1990	-162.66	36.71	79.96	-50.45	219.90	4.03	24.51	-290.84	-161.88	10.15	117.32	74.01	2633.66
1991	102.73	145.79	31.68	-25.99									
UP	28	23	27	26	19	21	24	23	14	22	27	29	
DOWN	14	19	15	16	22	20	17	18	27	19	14	12	
TOTALS	678.77	258.23	451.52	504.05	50.25	163.03	377.04	42.50	-482.99	413.04	407.96	650.72	

128

Only trade hour to hour during option expiration on Thursday and Friday.
Otherwise find the trend. Use short interest gathering and release dates

STRATEGY PLANNING & RECORD SECTION

ASPT
PYXS
VTEX

CONTENTS

PORTFOLIO AT START OF YEAR

DATE ACQUIRED	NO. OF SHARES	SECURITY	PRICE	TOTAL COST	PAPER PROFITS	PAPER LOSSES

ADDITIONAL PURCHASES

DATE ACQUIRED	NO. OF SHARES	SECURITY	PRICE	TOTAL COST	REASON FOR PURCHASE PRICE OBJECTIVE, ETC.

ADDITIONAL PURCHASES

DATE ACQUIRED	NO. OF SHARES	SECURITY	PRICE	TOTAL COST	REASON FOR PURCHASE PRICE OBJECTIVE, ETC.

ADDITIONAL PURCHASES

DATE ACQUIRED	NO. OF SHARES	SECURITY	PRICE	TOTAL COST	REASON FOR PURCHASE PRICE OBJECTIVE, ETC.

ADDITIONAL PURCHASES

DATE ACQUIRED	NO. OF SHARES	SECURITY	PRICE	TOTAL COST	REASON FOR PURCHASE PRICE OBJECTIVE, ETC.

SHORT-TERM TRANSACTIONS

Pages 135-140 can accompany next year's income tax return (Schedule D). Enter Transactions as completed to avoid last-minute pressures.

NO. OF SHARES	SECURITY	DATE ACQUIRED	DATE SOLD	SALES PRICE	COST	LOSS	GAIN

TOTALS: Carry over to next page

135

SHORT-TERM TRANSACTIONS (continued)

NO. OF SHARES	SECURITY	DATE ACQUIRED	DATE SOLD	SALES PRICE	COST	LOSS	GAIN
					TOTALS:		

SHORT-TERM TRANSACTIONS (continued)

NO. OF SHARES	SECURITY	DATE ACQUIRED	DATE SOLD	SALES PRICE	COST	LOSS	GAIN
						TOTALS:	

SHORT-TERM TRANSACTIONS (continued)

NO. OF SHARES	SECURITY	DATE ACQUIRED	DATE SOLD	SALES PRICE	COST	LOSS	GAIN

TOTALS:

LONG-TERM TRANSACTIONS

Pages 135-140 can accompany next year's income tax return (Schedule D). Enter Transactions as completed to avoid last-minute pressures.

NO. OF SHARES	SECURITY	DATE ACQUIRED	DATE SOLD	SALES PRICE	COST	LOSS	GAIN

TOTALS: Carry over to next page

LONG-TERM TRANSACTIONS

NO. OF SHARES	SECURITY	DATE ACQUIRED	DATE SOLD	SALES PRICE	COST	LOSS	GAIN
					TOTALS:		

PORTFOLIO AT END OF YEAR

DATE ACQUIRED	NO. OF SHARES	SECURITY	PRICE	TOTAL COST	PAPER PROFITS	PAPER LOSSES

INTEREST/DIVIDENDS RECEIVED DURING YEAR

AMOUNT	STOCK/BOND	FIRST QUARTER		SECOND QUARTER		THIRD QUARTER		FOURTH QUARTER	
		$		$		$		$	

INTEREST/DIVIDENDS RECEIVED DURING YEAR

AMOUNT	STOCK/BOND	FIRST QUARTER		SECOND QUARTER		THIRD QUARTER		FOURTH QUARTER	
		$		$		$		$	

BROKERAGE ACCOUNT DATA

	MARGIN INTEREST	TRANSFER TAXES	CAPITAL ADDED	CAPITAL WITHDRAWN
JAN				
FEB				
MAR				
APR				
MAY				
JUNE				
JUL				
AUG				
SEP				
OCT				
NOV				
DEC				

PORTFOLIO PRICE RECORD

Place original purchase price above stock name

STOCKS / Week Ending	1	2	3	4	5	6	7	8	Dow Jones Industrial Average	Net Change For Week
JANUARY 3										
10										
17										
24										
31										
FEBRUARY 7										
14										
21										
28										
MARCH 6										
13										
20										
27										
APRIL 3										
10										
17										
24										
MAY 1										
8										
15										
22										
29										
JUNE 5										
12										
19										
26										

Enter weekly closing prices for stocks in your portfolio

STOCKS Week Ending	9	10	11	12	13	14	15	16	17	18
JANUARY 3										
10										
17										
24										
31										
FEBRUARY 7										
14										
21										
28										
MARCH 6										
13										
20										
27										
APRIL 3										
10										
17										
24										
MAY 1										
8										
15										
22										
29										
JUNE 5										
12										
19										
26										

PORTFOLIO PRICE RECORD

Place original purchase price above stock name

STOCKS Week Ending	1	2	3	4	5	6	7	8	Dow Jones Industrial Average	Net Change For Week
JULY 3										
10										
17										
24										
31										
AUGUST 7										
14										
21										
28										
SEPTEMBER 4										
11										
18										
25										
OCTOBER 2										
9										
16										
23										
30										
NOVEMBER 6										
13										
20										
27										
DECEMBER 4										
11										
18										
25										

Enter weekly closing prices for stocks in your portfolio

STOCKS / Week Ending	9	10	11	12	13	14	15	16	17	18
JULY 3										
10										
17										
24										
31										
AUGUST 7										
14										
21										
28										
SEPTEMBER 4										
11										
18										
25										
OCTOBER 2										
9										
16										
23										
30										
NOVEMBER 6										
13										
20										
27										
DECEMBER 4										
11										
18										
25										

WEEKLY INDICATOR DATA (First Half)

Week Ending	Dow Jones Industrial Average	Net Change For Week	Net Change On Friday	Net Change Next Monday	S & P Or NYSE Comp.	NYSE Advances	NYSE Declines	New Highs	New Lows		90-Day Treas. Rate	30-Year AAA Rate
JANUARY 3												
10												
17												
24												
31												
FEBRUARY 7												
14												
21												
28												
MARCH 6												
13												
20												
27												
APRIL 3												
10												
17												
24												
MAY 1												
8												
15												
22												
29												
JUNE 5												
12												
19												
26												

See instructions on page 150

148

WEEKLY INDICATOR DATA (Second Half)

Week Ending	Dow Jones Industrial Average	Net Change For Week	Net Change On Friday	Net Change Next Monday	S & P Or NYSE Comp.	NYSE Ad-vances	NYSE De-clines	New Highs	New Lows		90-Day Treas. Rate	30-Year AAA Rate
3												
10												
17												
24												
31												
7												
14												
21												
28												
4												
11												
18												
25												
2												
9												
16												
23												
30												
6												
13												
20												
27												
4												
11												
18												
25												

See instructions on page 150

MONTHLY INDICATOR DATA

MONTH	DIJA Next To Last Day Prev. Mo.	DIJA Fourth Trading Day	Point Change These 5 Days	Point Change Rest Of Mo.	% Change Whole Period	% Change Your Stocks	Prime Rate	Trade Deficit $ Bil.	CPI % Change	% Unemployment Rate
JAN										
FEB										
MAR										
APR										
MAY										
JUN										
JUL										
AUG										
SEP										
OCT										
NOV										
DEC										

INSTRUCTIONS:

Weekly Indicator Data (page 148-149). Keeping data on several indicators may give you a better feel of the market. In addition to the closing DJIA and its net change for the week, post the net change for Friday's Dow and also the following Monday's. Watching the "down-on-Friday/down-on-Monday" phenomenon is fascinating. (See page 118 and also page 119.) Tracking either of the S&P or NYSE composites, and advances and declines, will help prevent the Dow from misleading you. New highs and new lows are also useful indicators. All these weekly figures appear in weekend papers or Barron's. Data for 90-day Treasury Rate and 30-year AAA Bond Rate are quite important to track short-and-long-term interest rates. These figures are available from:

> Weekly U.S. Financial Data
> Federal Reserve Bank of St. Louis
> P.O. Box 442
> St. Louis, MO 63166

Monthly Indicator Data. The purpose of the first four columns is to enable you to track (and possibly take advantage of) the market's bullish bias early in the month (see page 54, 56 and 120). Prime Rate, Trade Deficit, Consumers Price Index and Unemployment Rate are worthwhile indicators to follow. Or, readers may wish to use those columns for other data.

IF YOU DON'T PROFIT FROM YOUR INVESTMENT MISTAKES–SOMEONE ELSE WILL

No matter how much we may deny it, almost every successful person in Wall Street pays a great deal of attention to trading suggestions—especially when they come from "the right sources."

One of the hardest things to learn is to distinguish between good tips and bad ones. Usually the best tips have a logical reason back of them, which accompanies the tip. Poor tips generally have no reason to support them.

The important thing to remember is that the market discounts. It does not review, it does not reflect. The Street's real interest in "tips," inside information, buying and selling suggestions, and everything else of this kind, emanates from a desire to find out just what the market has on hand to discount. The process of finding out involves separating the wheat from the chaff—and there is plenty of chaff.

How To Make Use Of Stock "Tips"

1. The source should be **reliable**. (By listing all "tips" and suggestions on a Performance Record of Recommendations, such as below, and then periodically evaluating the outcomes, you will soon know the "batting average" of your sources.)

2. The story should make sense. Would the merger violate anti-trust laws? Are there too many computers on the market already? How many years will it take to become profitable?

3. The stock should not have had a recent sharp run-up. Otherwise, the story may already be discounted and confirmation or denial in the press would most likely be accompanied by a sell-off in the stock.

PERFORMANCE RECORD OF RECOMMENDATIONS

STOCK RECOMMENDED	BY WHOM	DATE	PRICE	REASON FOR RECOMMENDATION	SUBSEQUENT ACTION OF STOCK

G.M. LOEB'S "BATTLE PLAN" FOR INVESTMENT SURVIVAL

LIFE IS CHANGE: Nothing can ever be the same a minute from now as it was a minute ago. Everything you own is changing in price and value. You can find the last price of an active security on the stock ticker, but you cannot find the *next* price anywhere. The value of your money is changing. Even the value of your home is changing, though no one walks in front of it with a sandwich board constantly posting the changes.

RECOGNIZE CHANGE: Your basic objective should be to profit from change. The art of investing is being able to recognize change and to adjust investment goals accordingly.

WRITE THINGS DOWN: You will score more investment success and avoid more investment failures if you write things down. Very few investors have the drive and inclination to do this.

KEEP A CHECKLIST: If you aim to improve your investment results, try to get into the habit of keeping a checklist on every issue you consider buying. Before making a commitment, it will pay you to write down the answers to at least some basic questions—How much am I investing in this company? How much do I think I can make? How much do I have to risk? How long do I expect to take to reach my goal?

HAVE A SINGLE RULING REASON: Above all, writing things down is the best way to find "the ruling reason." When all is said and done, there is invariably a single reason that stands out above all others why a particular security transaction can be expected to show a profit. All too often many relatively unimportant statistics are allowed to obscure this single important point.

Anyone of a dozen factors may be the point of a particular purchase or sale. It could be a technical reason—a coming increase in earnings or dividend not yet discounted in the market price—a change of management—a promising new product—an expected improvement in the market's valuation of earnings—or many others. But, in any given case, one of these factors will almost certainly be more important than all the rest put together.

CLOSING OUT A COMMITMENT: If you have a loss in your stocks, the solution is automatic, provided you decide what to do at the time you buy. Otherwise, the question divides itself into two parts. Are we in a bull or bear market? Few of us really know until it is too late. For the sake of the record, if you think it is a bear market, just put that consideration first and sell as much as your conviction suggests and your nature allows.

If you think it is a bull market, or at least a market where some stocks move up, some mark time and only a few decline, do not sell unless:

(1) You see a bear market ahead.

(2) You see trouble for a particular company in which you own shares.

(3) Time and circumstances have turned up a new and seemingly far better buy than the issue you like least in your list.

(4) Your shares stop going up and start going down.

A subsidiary question is, which stock to sell first? Two further observations may help here:

(5) Do not sell solely because you think a stock is "overvalued."

(6) If you want to sell some of your stocks and not all, in most cases it is better to go against your emotional inclinations and sell first the issues with losses, small profits or none at all, the weakest, the most disappointing actors, etc.

Mr. Loeb is the author of *The Battle for Investment Survival*, Fraser, Box 494, Burlington, VT 05402

G. M. LOEB'S INVESTMENT SURVIVAL CHECKLIST

Objectives and Risks

Security		Price	Shares	Date

"Ruling reason" for commitment	Amount of commitment $
	% of my investment capital _____ %

Price objective	Est. time to achieve it	I will risk _____ points	Which would be $

Technical Position

Price action of stock:	Dow Jones Industrial Average

Price action of stock:

☐ hitting new highs   ☐ in a trading range

☐ pausing in an uptrend   ☐ moving up from low ground

☐ acting stronger than market   ☐ _____

Dow Jones Industrial Average

Trend of Market

Selected Yardsticks

	Price Range		Earnings Per Share Actual or Projected	Price/Earnings Ratio Actual or Projected
	High	Low		
Current Year				
Previous Year				
Merger Possibilities:				Years for earnings to double in past
Comment on Future:				Years for market price to double in past

Periodic Re-checks

Date	Stock Price	D.J.I.A.	Comment	Action taken, if any

Completed Transactions

Date closed	Period of time held	Profit or loss

Reason for profit or loss:

153

I.R.A.: THE MOST AWESOME
MASS INVESTMENT INCENTIVE EVER DEVISED

I.R.A. INVESTMENTS OF $2,000 A YEAR
COMPOUNDING AT VARIOUS RATES OF RETURN
FOR DIFFERENT PERIODS

Annual Rate	5 Yrs	10 Yrs	15 Yrs	20 Yrs	25 Yrs
1%	$10,304	$21,134	$ 32,516	$ 44,478	$ 57,050
2%	10,616	22,337	35,279	49,567	65,342
3%	10,937	23,616	38,314	55,353	75,106
4%	11,266	24,973	41,649	61,938	86,623
5%	11,604	26,414	45,315	69,439	100,227
6%	11,951	27,943	49,345	77,985	116,313
7%	12,307	29,567	53,776	87,730	135,353
8%	12,672	31,291	58,649	98,846	157,909
9%	13,047	33,121	64,007	111,529	184,648
10%	13,431	35,062	69,899	126,005	216,364
11%	13,826	37,123	76,380	142,530	253,998
12%	14,230	39,309	83,507	161,397	298,668
13%	14,645	41,629	91,343	182,940	351,700
14%	15,071	44,089	99,961	207,537	414,665
15%	15,508	46,699	109,435	235,620	489,424
16%	15,955	49,466	119,850	267,681	578,177
17%	16,414	52,400	131,298	304,277	683,525
18%	16,884	55,510	143,878	346,042	808,544
19%	17,366	58,807	157,700	393,695	956,861
20%	17,860	62,301	172,884	448,051	1,132,755

I.R.A. INVESTMENTS OF $2,000 A YEAR
COMPOUNDING AT VARIOUS RATES OF RETURN
FOR DIFFERENT PERIODS

Annual Rate	30 Yrs	35 Yrs	40 Yrs	45 Yrs	50 Yrs
1%	$ 70,265	$ 84,154	$ 98,750	$ 114,092	$ 130,216
2%	82,759	101,989	123,220	146,661	172,542
3%	98,005	124,552	155,327	191,003	232,362
4%	116,657	153,197	197,653	251,741	317,548
5%	139,522	189,673	253,680	335,370	439,631
6%	167,603	236,242	328,095	451,016	615,512
7%	202,146	295,827	427,219	611,504	869,972
8%	244,692	372,204	559,562	834,852	1,239,344
9%	297,150	470,249	736,584	1,146,372	1,776,882
10%	361,887	596,254	973,704	1,581,591	2,560,599
11%	441,826	758,329	1,291,654	2,190,338	3,704,672
12%	540,585	966,926	1,718,285	3,042,435	5,376,041
13%	662,630	1,235,499	2,290,972	4,235,612	7,818,486
14%	813,474	1,581,346	3,059,817	5,906,488	11,387,509
15%	999,914	2,026,691	4,091,908	8,245,795	16,600,747
16%	1,230,323	2,600,054	5,476,957	11,519,435	24,210,705
17%	1,515,008	3,337,989	7,334,781	16,097,540	35,309,434
18%	1,866,637	4,287,298	9,825,183	22,494,522	51,478,901
19%	2,300,775	5,507,829	13,160,993	31,424,150	75,006,500
20%	2,836,516	7,076,019	17,625,259	43,875,144	109,193,258

1993 STRATEGY CALENDAR
(Option expiration dates encircled)

	MONDAY	TUESDAY	WEDNESDAY	THURSDAY	FRIDAY	SAT	SUN
JANUARY	28	29	30	31	1 JANUARY New Year's Day	2	3
	4	5	6	7	8	9	10
	11	12	13	14	(15)	16	17
	18 Martin Luther King Day	19	20	21	22	23	24
	25	26	27	28	29	30	31
FEBRUARY	1 FEBRUARY	2	3	4	5	6	7
	8	9	10	11	12 Lincoln's Birthday	13	14
	15 Presidents' Day	16	17	18	(19)	20	21
	22	23	24 Ash Wednesday	25	26	27	28
MARCH	1 MARCH	2	3	4	5	6	7
	8	9	10	11	12	13	14
	15	16	17 St. Patrick's Day	18	(19)	20	21
	22	23	24	25	26	27	28
	29	30	31	1 APRIL	2	3	4
APRIL	5	6 Passover	7	8	9 Good Friday	10	11 Easter
	12	13	14	15	(16)	17	18
	19	20	21	22	23	24	25
	26	27	28	29	30	1 MAY	2
MAY	3	4	5	6	7	8	9 Mother's Day
	10	11	12	13	14	15	16
	17	18	19	20	(21)	22	23
	24	25	26	27	28	29	30
JUNE	31 Memorial Day	1 JUNE	2	3	4	5	6
	7	8	9	10	11	12	13
	14	15	16	17	(18)	19	20 Father's Day
	21	22	23	24	25	26	27

1993 STRATEGY CALENDAR
(Option expiration dates encircled)

MONDAY	TUESDAY	WEDNESDAY	THURSDAY	FRIDAY	SAT	SUN	
28	29	30	1 JULY	2	3	4 Independence Day	JULY
5	6	7	8	9	10	11	JULY
12	13	14	15	(16)	17	18	JULY
19	20	21	22	23	24	25	JULY
26	27	28	29	30	31	1 AUGUST	JULY
2	3	4	5	6	7	8	AUGUST
9	10	11	12	13	14	15	AUGUST
16	17	18	19	(20)	21	22	AUGUST
23	24	25	26	27	28	29	AUGUST
30	31	1 SEPTEMBER	2	3	4	5	SEPTEMBER
6 Labor Day	7	8	9	10	11	12	SEPTEMBER
13	14	15	16 Rosh Hashana	(17)	18	19	SEPTEMBER
20	21	22	23	24	25 Yom Kippur	26	SEPTEMBER
27	28	29	30	1 OCTOBER	2	3	OCTOBER
4	5	6	7	8	9	10	OCTOBER
11	12 Columbus Day	13	14	(15)	16	17	OCTOBER
18	19	20	21	22	23	24	OCTOBER
25	26	27	28	29	30	31	OCTOBER
1 NOVEMBER	2 Election Day	3	4	5	6	7	NOVEMBER
8	9	10	11 Veteran's Day	12	13	14	NOVEMBER
15	16	17	18	(19)	20	21	NOVEMBER
22	23	24	25 Thanksgiving	26	27	28	NOVEMBER
29	30	1 DECEMBER	2	3	4	5	DECEMBER
6	7	8	9 Hanukkah	10	11	12	DECEMBER
13	14	15	16	(17)	18	19	DECEMBER
20	21	22	23	24	25 Christmas	26	DECEMBER
27	28	29	30	31			DECEMBER

MARKET PROBABILITY CALENDAR 1992

The chance of the market rising on any trading day of the year.

(Based on the number of times the market rose on a particular trading day during May 1952-April 1991)

Date	Jan.	Feb.	Mar.	Apr.	May	June	July	Aug.	Sept.	Oct.	Nov.	Dec.
1	H	S	S	59.0	51.3	53.8	64.1	S	61.5	46.2	S	46.2
2	48.7	S	66.7	53.8	S	53.8	69.2	S	61.5	71.8	66.7	53.8
3	74.3	53.8	64.1	51.3	S	56.4	H	53.8	59.0	S	56.4	61.5
4	S	56.4	56.4	S	71.8	66.7	S	41.0	46.2	S	74.3	61.5
5	S	46.2	51.3	S	66.7	51.3	S	51.3	S	59.0	43.6	S
6	53.8	48.7	43.6	51.3	51.3	S	56.4	53.8	S	66.7	56.4	S
7	53.8	48.7	S	59.0	51.3	S	61.5	59.0	H	53.8	S	43.6
8	43.6	S	S	64.1	48.7	48.7	59.0	S	48.7	53.8	S	51.3
9	46.2	S	56.4	69.2	S	33.3	59.0	S	43.6	38.5	61.5	56.4
10	51.3	35.9	61.5	51.3	S	66.7	48.7	41.0	48.7	S	69.2	51.3
11	S	41.0	51.3	S	43.6	59.0	S	56.4	56.4	S	64.1	43.6
12	S	56.4	64.1	S	48.7	51.3	S	43.6	S	38.5	46.2	S
13	56.4	48.7	43.6	51.3	41.0	S	35.9	56.4	S	43.6	46.2	S
14	61.5	48.7	S	59.0	51.3	S	66.7	56.4	43.6	41.0	S	48.7
15	61.5	S	S	59.0	48.7	56.4	53.8	S	51.3	41.0	S	51.3
16	53.8	S	56.4	59.0	S	56.4	53.8	S	46.2	41.0	43.6	51.3
17	53.8	H	56.4	H	S	48.7	53.8	51.3	48.7	S	61.5	48.7
18	S	46.2	64.1	S	33.3	48.7	S	51.3	43.6	S	48.7	48.7
19	S	41.0	51.3	S	48.7	53.8	S	43.6	S	56.4	69.2	S
20	56.4	51.3	48.7	48.7	53.8	S	35.9	56.4	S	46.2	66.7	S
21	43.6	51.3	S	46.2	43.6	S	53.8	41.0	53.8	46.2	S	51.3
22	43.6	S	S	46.2	48.7	56.4	48.7	S	53.8	38.5	S	46.2
23	69.2	S	46.2	41.0	S	46.2	46.2	S	53.8	46.2	61.5	38.5
24	61.5	28.2	53.8	56.4	S	35.9	41.0	46.2	51.3	S	71.8	61.5
25	S	43.6	35.9	S	H	48.7	S	46.2	53.8	S	56.4	H
26	S	56.4	56.4	S	46.2	51.3	S	38.5	S	51.3	H	S
27	43.6	51.3	59.0	64.1	38.5	S	53.8	53.8	S	53.8	53.8	S
28	56.4	61.5	S	43.6	53.8	S	56.4	51.3	59.0	56.4	S	64.1
29	41.0	S	S	38.5	59.0	53.8	51.3	S	41.0	53.8	S	53.8
30	61.5		33.3	59.0	S	59.0	64.1	S	41.0	51.3	56.4	66.7
31	64.1		38.5		S		66.7	74.3		S		74.3

MARKET PROBABILITY CHART

The chances of the market rising on any trading day of the year.

(Based on the number of times the market rose on a particular trading day during the period May 1952-April 1991)

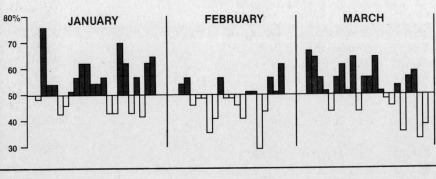

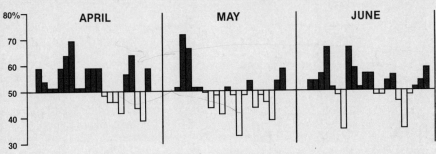

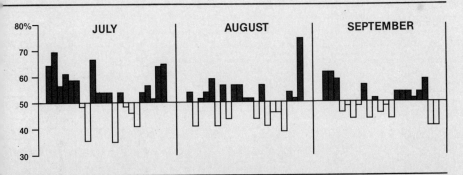

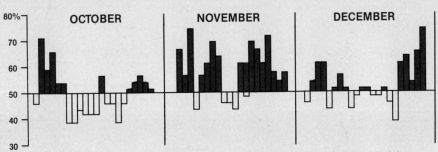

Shows the usual number of trading days in each month (Saturdays, Sundays and holidays excluded).

FINANCIAL DIRECTORY
Broker, Lawyer, Accountant, Banker, etc.

#371

98491950

NAME AND ADDRESS	AREA CODE	NUMBER
When a market is o/b or o/s the specialists will wait for an event that will trigger the price of stocks in the opposite direction and the accelerate the move.		
Determine sentiment from newsletters & charts		
Overbought / oversold condition determined by Option Open Interest		